BETTER
TOGETHER

HOW TO SUPPORT THE
PROACTIVE MENTAL HEALTH OF
FAMILY, FRIENDS AND COWORKERS

JUDD ALLEN, Ph.D.

Human Resources Institute, LLC
www.healthyculture.com
151 Dunder Road
Burlington, Vermont 05401 USA
JuddA@healthyculture.com
(802) 862-8855

Ordering Information
Quantity sales. Special discounts are available on quantity purchases by organizations,
associations, and others. For details, contact the publisher.
Library of Congress Cataloging-in-Publication Data
Names: Allen, Judd, 1958-author.
Better Together: How to Support the Proactive Mental Health of Family, Friends and Coworkers
Description: Burlington, Vermont: HealthyCulture.com [2023] | Includes bibliographical
references.
Identifiers: eBook ISBN 978-0-941703-48-2; paperback ISBN 978-0-941703-47-5
Hardcover/Cloth ISBN 978-0-941703-49-9
Subjects: NONFICTION/Self-Help/Mental Health

Cover photograph of Judd Allen by Karen Pike of www.kpikephoto.com.

Contents

Acknowledgments

My father, Robert Allen, Ph.D., inspired my interest in supportive cultural environments. This book is a tribute to his life's work.

I would like to thank my colleagues, Don Ardell, Michael Arloski, David Ballard, Craig Becker, Jim Carman, Bill Hettler, Joe Leutzinger, Tad Mitchell, Michael O'Donnell, Gillian Pieper, Kay Ryan, Samia Simurro, Marie-Josee Shaar, Ewa Stelmasiak, Elaine Sullivan, and Jack Travis. These leaders share a vision that includes both kindness and flourishing.

My close friends and family generously provided their feedback. Mollie Allen, Richard Blount, Jonathan Sands, and Mary Sochet were a big help.

Better Together benefited from thoughtful editing by Colleen Webb.

Statement About Inclusive Language

This is a book about mental health and emotional well-being. We recognize that humans are extraordinarily diverse in identity and sexual orientation. The English language should honor that diversity. In this book, I use gender-neutral language. Where, for example, you may have seen he/she, I'm going to use they them.

Chapter 1
Helping Family, Friends and Coworkers to Flourish

To flourish
1: to grow luxuriantly: THRIVE
2a: to achieve success: PROSPER
b: to be in a state of activity or production
c: to reach a height of development or influence
"FLOURISH." MERRIAM-WEBSTER.COM DICTIONARY

THERE IS A riveting, inspiring story to write about how you supported a friend, family member or coworker to dramatically reduce mental illness and to increase overall mental well-being. This page turner is a story about helping to set proactive mental health goals and then supporting their achievement. The story is about your family member, friend, neighbor, or coworker achieving lasting and positive changes in attitudes and behaviors.

This is not a story about therapy or mental health treatment, although your peer may seek such professional assistance. This is a story about preventing mental illness and achieving well-being. Flourishing is a team sport. We do this together. You can help a peer to flourish by achieving important proactive mental health goals, such as those centered around:

- **Safety**—economic, physical, and emotional security
- **Connection**—positive and empowering relationships among coworkers, immediate supervisors/managers, housemates, family, and friends
- **Purpose**—meaning at work and outside of work
- **Presence**—mindfulness, inner peace, and an enjoyment of the here and now
- **Health Behavior**—preventive medicine, physical activity, and healthy eating
- **Adaptability**—personal growth, goal achievement and affirmative responses to change

The goal of *Better Together* is to empower you to provide effective peer support. The chapters in this book define key support strategies, provide measurement tools, and highlight opportunities for constructive change.

Preventing Mental Illness

Struggles with mental health are pervasive and highly consequential. Approximately one half of our peers (46.4%)

are likely to experience mental illness in their lifetime. Twenty-one percent of U.S. adults—that's 52.9 million people—experienced mental illness in 2020. Every year 12 billion working days are lost due to mental illness. Mental illness among parents is having a devastating effect on children and families.

Current approaches to mental illness treatment are very costly. However, these approaches only address the needs of those people currently afflicted with mental illness. Ideally, we would treat mental illness and increase mental well-being. Little is being done to prevent mental illness, and even less is being done to promote robust mental health by living productive, happy, and healthy lives.

Promoting the proactive mental health of your peers is an important strategy for reducing the likelihood that your peers will suffer from mental illness. We need each other's help because mental health professionals cannot treat all those afflicted with anxiety, depression, alcoholism, substance abuse, dissociative disorders, eating disorders, obsessive compulsive disorders, paranoia, post-traumatic stress disorder, psychosis, and schizophrenia. For too many of us, mental health treatment is out of reach.

Shifting the culture towards proactive mental health begins with an agreement that our current approach, which focuses almost exclusively on treating mental illness through therapy and drugs, cannot address the conditions needed for people to be resilient and thrive. When it comes to those suffering with mental illness, treatment is the right thing to do and important. However, prevention is the preferred approach for creating a state of flourishing. We need to proactively support mental health by adopting practices that lower the risks and speed recovery from mental illness. Helping your friends, family, and coworkers to achieve strong mental health is paramount.

Promoting proactive mental health among your peers is a powerful upstream approach to addressing the challenges and opportunities of mental illness and overall well-being. Mental health encapsulates more than just not being sick. True mental health encompasses the needs of the whole person to achieve optimal quality of life. Proactive mental health embraces strategies that make us more resilient and help us to quickly recover from mental illness.

The urge to be helpful is instinctive. The current mental health crisis threatens our own well-being and the well-being of all those in our social networks. Fortunately, when it comes to mental health, there is a great deal we can do to both prevent mental illness and promote overall well-being. This book is about supporting the most powerful proactive mental health attitudes and behaviors.

Shattering Cultural Myths about Mental Illness and Health

Better Together challenges several widely held cultural beliefs about mental health and illness. Debunking the following myths jump-starts our journey toward proactive mental health:

Cultural myth: Few people experience mental illness.

Fact: Roughly 21 percent of people are currently experiencing mental illness. Nearly 50 percent of people will experience such challenges over the course of their lifetime.

Cultural myth: There is little that anyone can do to reduce the risk of mental illness.

Fact: While it is true that we all have different predispositions to mental illnesses, many attitudes and behaviors can dramatically reduce the risk. In this sense, mental health challenges are like cancer and heart disease.

Cultural myth: Mental health is merely the absence of mental illness.

Fact: Mental health is a quality-of-life concept directed at optimal emotional and mental well-being. Health is not just about the avoidance of illness. It also includes enjoying optimal well-being. It is also true that some people can have mental illness and still enjoy other aspects of their lives where they are experiencing high mental well-being.

Cultural myth: Mental illness is exclusively an individual problem.

Fact: Unsupportive cultural environments play a major role in undermining peoples' mental health. An example is how stressors at work and at home can disrupt healthy sleep. In addition, current cultural norms make seeking mental health treatment uncomfortable for some people. We need to find or create cultural environments at work, at home, and in the community that support proactive mental health attitudes and behaviors. We also need a stronger cultural norm for getting help.

Cultural myth: Effective peer support is as simple as being a good listener.

Fact: While it is true that listening is helpful, there are additional peer support strategies that greatly enhance the benefits of such support. For example, we can assist our peers in identifying their goals; locating role models who have achieved similar goals under similar circumstances; and developing strategies for overcoming barriers to change.

Cultural myth: Peer support only benefits the person receiving support.

Fact: Peer support is beneficial for both the person giving support and the person receiving support. Providing peer support raises self-esteem and builds one's social network. When we assist others, we reinforce our own commitment to healthy living. We also get an opportunity to deepen our understanding of personal change.

Peer support fortifies our mental health. Providing such support strengthens our social connections with friends, neighbors, family, and coworkers. Citing over 100 epidemiological studies, cardiologist Dean Ornish summarized overwhelming evidence that people with close relationships are more likely to choose life-enhancing behaviors rather than self-destructive ones. Peer support helps us survive and thrive.

Cultural myth: Peer support undermines individual initiative.

Fact: To make personal changes, people need to want to change. Fortunately, most people already have personal mental health goals, and they may have already attempted to change. But most health resolutions have a short lifespan. Your support increases the likelihood that your peer will succeed in the long term.

Cultural myth: Peer support is a poor substitute for professional support.

Fact: Mental health specialists are trained to uncover subconscious and biological conditions. Peers can assist in carrying out recommendations from these health professionals and they are well positioned to do so because they are right in the mix of day-to-day activities. People who receive peer support are much more likely to maintain their personal change goals. Our friends, family and coworkers are eyewitnesses and companions for lasting and positive change. Peer support can increase the benefit of professional mental health support.

Your Peer Support Role

Peer support is assistance provided by coworkers, friends, family, and neighbors. It can be practical assistance such as sharing equipment and covering for childcare. Peer support also comes in the form of emotional assistance, such as offering sympathy and being present.

Providing effective peer support isn't complicated. You can increase the quality and amount of support you offer by adding strategies to your peer support toolkit. This book takes a chapter-by-chapter deep dive into seven core peer support skills:

1. **Building a solid foundation for your support.** This includes your offer of assistance, establishing trust, and planning follow-up.

2. **Setting goals.** The focus is on clarifying proactive mental health goals, exploring related scientific knowledge, and tailoring personal goals. You learn to set both short- and long-term goals.

3. **Identifying role models.** You learn to help your peer find people who have achieved similar goals under similar circumstances. Role models can share about what worked, what challenges were overcome, and other tips that might be useful.

4. **Eliminating barriers to change.** You learn to identify potential physical and psychological barriers and help your peer develop strategies to break down these barriers and overcome them. The approach to barriers is positive, with an emphasis on existing strengths and finding resources needed for success.

5. **Locating supportive environments.** You learn to help your peer examine physical and social environments (at work, at home and in the community) to determine how they might support or undermine success. You assist your peer in developing strategies to reduce contact with less supportive environments and to increase contact with the environments that better support proactive mental health goals.

6. **Working through and/or avoiding setbacks.** No one wants to get off track and fail to achieve personal change goals, but challenges are common. You help your peer devise strategies to avoid high-risk situations for setbacks and plans for handling relapse. Your peer will be in position to learn from setbacks and to make appropriate adjustments.

7. **Celebrating success.** Most successes go unrecognized. This is unfortunate because rewards reinforce change. You and your peer will identify occasions to celebrate progress as well as determine the most meaningful way to make success count.

Your offer to assist is a tremendous gift. If you fortify your peer support efforts with some of the techniques on the following pages, your kindness and understanding can make a substantial difference. Your peer will be more likely to be successful and you will benefit from providing that support.

Case Stories about Peer Support and Proactive Mental Health

The following stories highlight some of the many opportunities for putting peer support and proactive mental health to work. The first story about Lamonte and Tyron incorporates the full range of proactive mental health and peer support concepts. The subsequent stories illustrate the diverse relationships and challenges that can be addressed by combining peer support with proactive mental health goals.

Lamonte and Tyrone: Finding Renewal Amid Burnout

Most students know Lamonte as Mr. Washington. He teaches math at Martin Luther King Jr High. Most students know Tyrone as Mr. Wilson. He teaches American history. These long-time friends are among the few male teachers at their school. With over 20 years of experience each, they are also veteran teachers. They remain passionate about their work, but societal trends and changes in their local community have increased their concern for their students and taken a lot of the joy out of jobs that they loved.

Both teachers received *Better Together* from the school wellness program. The cover letter talked about preventing mental illness and improving overall well-being. It recommended reading the book with a coworker, friend, housemate, or family member. Lamonte and Tyrone decided to give it a try together. They hoped to learn more about mental health and how they could get out of their current funk. They set a goal to read one chapter a week and to get together to discuss what they had learned.

Lamonte and Tyrone talked about the *Better Together* chapter on goal setting. They answered the questions in the Proactive Mental Health Self-Assessment and discussed each of the six dimensions. Safety was an issue, as they were seeing more violence between students and in the broader community. Purpose was also a challenge as teaching math and history was now undermined by increased chaos in the school. Adaptability was another challenging proactive mental health dimension. The high level of adaptability that they took for granted earlier in their careers was now lacking due to ongoing stress and lower levels of personal energy.

They talked about the *Better Together* chapter on finding role models and were short on good candidates. Did they know teachers that were thriving now? If there was such a teacher, they were keeping a low profile during a time when complaining had become the norm. They decided to reflect on past role models. They even found examples of times in their own lives when they were good role models for their current selves.

They talked about the chapter on lowering barriers. One barrier was the high level of noise in the school. Maybe they could enlist the support of other teachers and students in lowering the decibels. Were there ways to better soundproof doors? Could they refurbish the teacher's lounge and make it a refuge?

They talked about the chapter on supportive people and places. The school culture needed attention. People had grown apart. The high turnover among staff and teachers left many people feeling like they worked among strangers. Lamonte and Tyrone decided to work with the administration to reinvigorate mechanisms for welcoming and mentoring new people.

They talked about the chapter on working through setbacks. What would they do on days when they were feeling low? Both teachers loved music. They decided to listen to their favorites or take a walk around the school grounds to lift their spirits. They agreed to check in with each other when they were feeling down.

They talked about the chapter on tracking progress

and celebrating success. For both teachers, the success of their students was paramount. They would make a special effort to honor student progress. They would also look for signs that the school was improving. Lower drop-out rates, higher test scores, and college acceptances were all to be celebrated.

Thanks to pairing up, Lamonte and Tyrone were on the way to a happier and healthier future. They were satisfied that they had covered important strategies for improving their mental health. They agreed that they could not have done this alone; their best ideas came from putting their heads together and challenging each other, just as they'd always done with students in the classroom.

Amelia and Callie: Exploring Sobriety

Amelia had known Callie since college, and they had been through a lot together. Callie noticed that her drinking had become problematic in recent years, affecting her ability to perform well at work and to be a good role model for her son. She asked Amelia for her support in exploring sobriety.

Amelia and Callie began by talking about their relationship, which sometimes involved meeting up for a drink. They needed new ways to connect. They agreed to meet once a week to walk and talk.

During their walks, they tackled many questions. Did Callie know if she needed to quit drinking or just cut back? Were there places and people that she needed to avoid? What places and relationships would be good alternatives?

Were there high-risk situations that should be managed or avoided altogether?

Callie decided she wanted to stop drinking. She knew she would sometimes be tempted to drink, so she and Amelia planned to check in by phone call or text message when that happened. Amelia was there to remind her of her progress. She never judged or criticized Callie for wanting a drink, but instead encouraged her to stick with her commitment.

As time passed, Callie became more comfortable without a drink. She developed a meditation practice to help her sit with her feelings, rather than reaching for alcohol when she was overwhelmed. She felt much better about the role modeling she was doing for her son.

Amelia could see how much happier her friend was. Although they no longer met up for drinks, the change brought Amelia and Callie closer together. She knew that Callie had worked hard to get to this point, and she was grateful to have been there to support her.

Zach and Joseph: Building Financial Responsibility

Zach had always been a protective big brother to Joseph. When he found out that his little brother was in financial trouble, he wanted to step in and help. Joseph had always been impulsive with his spending, and it had caught up with him. He was living paycheck to paycheck and was $50,000 in debt.

Out of respect for Joseph, Zach resisted the urge to jump in to fix things and instead let his brother know that he was there to help when he was ready. Several months passed before Joseph accepted that his financial situation was deteriorating beyond his ability to hide or control. He reached out to Zach to discuss how he could turn things around.

Zach didn't have any professional credentials in finance, but he was intentional with his own money and had developed good saving and spending habits. The brothers discussed many ways to approach Joseph's money problems, including hiring a debt counselor or financial planner.

Joseph was embarrassed by his situation and intimidated by the long path to financial responsibility. Zach recognized that his brother needed to hear some success stories to boost his morale and show him the way forward. They searched for an online support group, because anonymity was a priority. Joseph also found young, male influencers who had dug their way out of debt and shared openly about what they'd learned.

Zach and Joseph talked about ways to cut back on his expenses. They started with the easier ones, like eating out less, to build confidence and momentum for the harder ones, like getting a roommate and passing on expensive vacations with friends.

Zach checked in with Joseph regularly as he started to implement the changes. He helped Joseph stay accountable to his budget and his debt-repayment plan. Over the next year, Joseph's debts were shrinking, and he no longer lived paycheck to paycheck. Helping Joseph get his finances in order not only improved his financial situation, but it also deepened their relationship.

Jacob and Brina: Enduring Teen Struggles

Jacob is Brina's loving dad. Brina just turned 15 and is a sophomore in high school. Her main interests are volleyball, tennis, and dancing. She identifies as gay.

Brina does not feel safe at school where being gay is not accepted by many students and teachers. She is often taunted by other students on her walk to and from school. She has talked with her dad about this but asked that he not get involved.

Being gay leaves Brina's socially isolated. There are not many other kids her age who have come out. She's fine with hanging out with her straight peers, but the anti-gay atmosphere makes it hard for her to connect with them. She feels like an outsider.

Like many teenagers, Brina tends to go to bed very late. She spends many hours on social media. Getting up for school is a challenge. On the weekends she tries to catch up by sleeping until noon.

Jacob is concerned about Brina's well-being, and they talk weekly about how she's doing and what they might do to help alleviate some of her struggles. They tried to find a support group to join, but nothing was available where they live, and Brina didn't want the added attention that would come with her dad starting his own group. Instead, they discussed finding a role model for her, someone who has come out under similar circumstances. They decided to look online for potential role models because Brina's privacy is a priority.

Jacob and Brina realized that sports activities are

a shared passion and a strength, so Jacob committed to attending most of Brina's volleyball and tennis matches. He loves cheering his daughter on. They also joined club volleyball to extend the season. Weekend travel for club volleyball requires getting up early. Brina agreed to cut off screentime by 9 pm so she could get to sleep by 10. She wants to be alert for volleyball.

Being a teenager is not easy. Jacob and Brina check in daily. Brina knows that her dad will be available when she feels overwhelmed, and Jacob is on the lookout for ways to lighten the load and to help his daughter push through the challenges. They know that they are in this together.

Pamela and Suzanne: Navigating Divorce

Suzanne and Pamela had been close friends for years, so when Pamela started going through a divorce, Suzanne offered her support and encouragement. When Pamela was ready, she and Suzanne decided to meet in person once a week and check in by phone every day.

Suzanne and Pamela discussed her needs, including taking care of her mental health, building more social connections, and establishing financial independence. They created a list of activities to help Pamela cope with the transition. The list started out long: journaling, meditation, exercise, spending time in nature, improving sleep habits, socializing weekly with friends, finding a divorce support group, seeking employment assistance, and finding a financial advisor. Pamela felt overwhelmed, but Suzanne reminded her that she could and should move at her own pace.

They worked together to prioritize one item at a time, setting concrete goals so that Pamela's efforts were focused and effective. In their weekly check-ins, Pamela shared her progress and challenges. They problem solved together, and Pamela let Suzanne know when she was ready to tackle a new goal.

Over time, Pamela started to see progress. Focusing on her sleep and incorporating daily habits around exercise, time outside, and journaling helped her cope with emotional challenges. The social connections she found with her weekly get-togethers and her support group increased her sense of belonging and support. Pamela found a great role model in the leader of her support group. She became more optimistic about the new life she was cultivating, and she began to consider pursuing new hobbies and interests.

Pamela and Suzanne celebrated together when the divorce was finalized. It was more than a legal document—they celebrated how Pamela survived such a tumultuous situation and rose above it. They celebrated Suzanne's help and unconditional support, which were pivotal in Pamela's life-altering season. Their work together created a springboard for Pamela to bounce back from self-defeating emotions and to launch a bright future.

My Proactive Mental Health Story

Cultural support, mental health, and mental illness have been important topics in my life. Like me, many members of my immediate family are psychologists, social workers, and psychiatrists. My father, Robert Allen, Ph.D. attributed our family's passion for mental health to a lesson learned from his father, Ed Allen.

Ed was wounded in World War I. During his hospitalization, he became addicted to morphine. He was able to overcome his addiction but was unable to shake the war trauma he experienced. He spent his adult life in and out of mental health services, unable to work, and lived from disability checks. He was ashamed about his inability to hold a job.

Fortunately, Ed's spirits lifted when he reached retirement age and redefined himself as retired. This new retired status allowed him to face the world without shame. In my grandfather's time, the culture did not support people with mental illness, but it was supportive of retired men.

In my grandfather's story, my father recognized a significant connection between culture and mental illness. Like my father—also a psychologist—I have dedicated my life's work to creating supportive cultural environments for mental health.

Better Together is the culmination of more than sixty years of helping groups and organizations build caring communities. My father formed our company, the Human Resources Institute (HRI), in the 1960s. HRI has served more 1,000 government, business, educational, union, and health care organizations. Since my father's death in 1987, I have authored more than fifty books, book chapters, movies, and journal articles about creating supportive cultural environments.

In 2022, I wrote my first book on proactive mental health, *We Flourish*, to explain how executives, managers, and human resource professionals can create supportive workgroup and organizational cultures. *Better Together* focuses on the role of peers (friends, neighbors, coworkers, and family) in supporting proactive mental health. One of my first books, *Healthy Habits, Helpful Friends* (2008), focused on peer support for healthy lifestyles. *We Flourish* (2022) and *Healthy Habits, Helpful Friends* (2008) provide the foundation for *Better Together*.

The wellness and health promotion movements also provide a foundation for key ideas in *Better Together*. HRI assisted in the development of many of the early corporate wellness programs during the 1970s. Over the past fifty years, employers have been offering programs and services designed to support healthier lifestyles. The original wellness vision focused on both quality of life and avoiding health risks. These programs tended to focus on physical activity, health eating smoking cessation, and health screenings. The primary focus of wellness programs was the prevention of cardiovascular diseases, cancer, and premature death from all causes.

These workplace wellness programs did not focus specifically on mental health. However, the original wellness vision—that we can adopt attitudes and behaviors that help us to thrive—is a core premise of *Better Together*. Addressing mental illness and promoting mental well-being are highly consistent with the original wellness philosophy first articulated by visionaries like doctors Halbert Dunn, Donald Ardell, Bill Hettler, Robert Allen, and Jack Travis.

Both Leadership and Peer Support

In American culture, there is a tendency to emphasize the role of leadership in creating supportive cultures. There is little doubt that leaders can play important roles. I wrote my first book on mental health, *We Flourish,* with that goal in mind. The book explains how executives, managers, human resource professionals, and wellness champions can create workplace cultures that support proactive mental health.

However, I'm convinced that peer support from family, friends, neighbors, and coworkers can and should play a valuable role in supporting lasting and positive changes in attitudes and behavior. We need both leadership and peer support. Our peers are available to offer a lasting and effective support system. Such peer support can last a lifetime. Peer support is freely given and readily available. Long-term support is needed for lasting change. *Better Together* skills, offered in the following chapters, are likely to dramatically increase your ability to offer effective peer support.

Chapter 2

Building the Foundation for Peer Support

The thing that lies at the foundation of positive change,
the way I see it, is service to a fellow human being.

—LECH WALESA

SUCCESSFUL PEER SUPPORT requires a solid foundation. Such a foundation requires understanding and explaining peer support; establishing confidentiality; scheduling follow-up meetings; and explaining how your voluntary support fits with that offered by mental health professionals. A good foundation enhances trust and openness. Clarity about your approach will make your efforts more effective.

Many People Try to Change Without Adequate Support

When it comes to trying to achieve healthier habits, no one should feel alone. Each year approximately 80 percent of the adults in North America attempt to achieve behaviors that would support their mental health. These include attempts to be more physically active, improve sleep, eat healthier, and manage stress. The enthusiasm for self-improvement and self-preservation, combined with the ready availability of information on the benefits of healthy practices, appear to be making proactive mental health related behavior change attempts a common phenomenon.

The fact that we are attempting to change our unhealthy behavior is great mental health news. Motivation is essential to success, and we appear well motivated to address unhealthy and unsatisfactory aspects of our day-to-day behavior.

Unfortunately, most of these change efforts fail to succeed. And most people are trying to make these changes without sufficient support from housemates, family, friends, coworkers, and neighbors.

See for Yourself

Next time you are in a group of 10 or more people, ask for a show of hands...

Raise your hand if in the past year you attempted to change one or more health practices. This includes attempting to manage stress, improve friendships, eat

healthier, exercise, or anything else you might have done for a New Year's resolution or other motivation.

You are very likely to see a vast majority of hands go up.

Then privately, so as not to cause embarrassment, ask about success. How many people fully achieved their personal change goals? Listen to their experiences. You are very likely to hear about big plans and little progress. Most people will report that they did not fully achieve their intended goals for more than a brief time.

Clarifying Your Peer Support Role

Effective peer support has four qualities that tend to set it apart from other forms of informal and non-paid support:

- **Creating a safe and caring relationship for exploring personal proactive mental health goals.** This requires establishing trust and working to keep communications open, positive, and free from guilt.

- **Asking questions that are useful in planning long-term change.** This involves doing more listening than telling; asking for clarification; and reflecting upon what you hear. Effective peer support involves offering more thought-provoking questions than advice.

- **Seeking out resources for achieving proactive mental health goals.** You utilize your contacts and ingenuity to get useful information and to gain needed resources. You may, for example, join your peer in searching the Internet or attending a seminar. You may also join in brainstorming strategies for freeing time for pursuing proactive mental health goals.

- **Embracing the learning and growth that comes from someone's journey.** Your primary concern is avoiding negative judgements and, instead, supporting your peer in taking actions that are heartfelt and truly reflect personal choice.

Peer Support Is Not Professional Mental Health Support

As a peer, your role is different from that of a mental health professional. Unlike those in a professional helping role, you will not be compensated financially for your help. Whereas a therapist or psychiatrist is focused on identifying deeper psychological or physical causes underlying behavior, your support focuses on the practical aspects. You may help your peer find a professional if you encounter deeper and more mysterious problems that need attention.

Although teachers and personal coaches are professionals who guide people with their expertise in a particular area, you are not claiming to be a counseling or mental health expert. You will ask questions designed to guide your peer toward determining their best direction, rather than saying what you think is the best direction. Together you will seek out useful information from reliable sources.

Drawing Upon the Tradition of Mentoring

The mentor role has its origins in *The Odyssey*, Homer's ancient Greek epic poem. Odysseus, the king of Ithaca, had a problem. He was leaving to fight in the Trojan War and needed to find someone who could help his independent-minded son, Telemachus, learn to be a king. Odysseus chose a man named Mentor because he saw that Mentor had special skills.

Recognizing that his personal experience would have limited value, Mentor taught Telemachus by asking questions. Mentor also saw the value of encouraging Telemachus to pursue his national inclinations. He also encouraged Telemachus to change course based on what he was learning. Mentor's strategy worked. Telemachus went on to become a helpful son and leader.

As in *The Odyssey*, offering effective peer support does not require direct personal experience with a particular proactive mental health goal. Instead, it occurs through the mutual embrace of the learning and growth of a personal journey. Assistance comes primarily in offering thought-provoking questions rather than advice. You recognize that knowledge unfolds during the process of change. The mentor has faith that their peer can, and most often will, find the best path to their own proactive mental health.

Establishing Trust

Supporting successful mental health goals usually requires a high level of trust. For many of us, this prerequisite can be unsettling. Weren't we taught as children not to trust others? Weren't we taught that change was somehow more valuable if we could claim that we had "done it all by ourselves"? Didn't we learn somewhere that we should keep our personal business to ourselves, and that needing others was a sign of personal weakness?

As it turns out, many of these fundamental childhood lessons about distrusting others and not needing them undermine successful behavior change. We need to break out of this dysfunctional attitude about establishing and maintaining trust.

To make the concept of trust more manageable, it is helpful to break it down into types of trust. The four Cs of trust are:

- **Contextual Trust**
- **Communication Trust**
- **Contractual Trust**
- **Competence Trust**

Contextual Trust

Contextual trust means that our relationship with our peer has a broad basis of familiarity. As we get to know the history and special interests of others, we can begin to appreciate and trust them more. Sometimes this form of trust is established through years of shared life experiences. This could be true of family members or longtime friends. However, all too often, people spend years working and living side by side without really knowing very much about the others' range of experiences. At work, for example, we may know our peers' specific task or job responsibility without knowing anything about their family life, hobbies, and personal aspirations.

When thinking about contextual trust, think about the relationship-building skills of successful salespeople. A successful salesperson, sitting down with a customer, does not immediately make sales pitches unless the customer insists. Instead, they open with a discussion of common personal interests such as hobbies, family responsibilities or sports. They know that to negotiate the best business deal, the two parties must build trust. In a similar way, we should not leap into giving or getting support for health behavior change. First establish a relationship.

By broadening the basis of a relationship, we will feel more comfortable expressing our true feelings and be better able to give and receive constructive feedback. With mutual and broader knowledge of one another, the person receiving the feedback is more likely to experience feedback as having been given in the spirit of helpfulness. In contrast, if all we know about a person is related to one unhealthy behavior, then feedback about that behavior often feels like a criticism of the whole person. When constructive suggestions or probing questions are offered in the context of a broad relationship, it's less likely to feel like a criticism.

Activity for Establishing Contextual Trust

One way to quickly establish contextual trust is to take turns answering "getting to know you" questions. You may want to use the following questions. Try to share meaningful personal experiences and perspectives without venturing into what should really remain private. Sharing such experiences should be optional – answer only those questions you feel comfortable with.

Tell each other about:

- Places you have lived

- A major change you have made

- Something that would help anyone understand you better

- A childhood experience that has had a lasting effect on you

- A person who has had an important impact on you

- How you chose your present work

- An experience in the last year or two that made a significant impression on you

- An obstacle you've overcome

- A significant personal achievement

- Your hobbies and special interests

Communication Trust

The second "C" of trust, communication trust, refers to the willingness to disclose relevant information. It also refers to using your peer's personal information in a considerate way. When it comes to giving and receiving support for lasting behavior change, accurate and complete information is essential. If you withhold your true feelings, the quality and quantity of support is undermined. In contrast, when communication trust is high, information flows freely. There are five key concepts that build – or detract from – your communication trust:

Confidentiality Agreements

Agreements about privacy help to build trust by outlining how and when it is appropriate to share personal information with others. When you are supporting a health behavior goal, there will be times when it could be useful to get input from outside sources. To maintain communication trust, you must share information only in a way that has been previously agreed to.

Establish your confidentiality guidelines early. Establish broad guidelines and then check in if unanticipated situations arise. You may want to add a couple of special situations in which personal beliefs, rules or laws dictate the disclosure of information. For example, if you were working with a school bus driver, you might want to state up front that if the conversation indicates that alcohol or other drugs are being used at work, you will find it necessary to contact the employee assistance program or other authorities about the need for assistance.

The key is to discuss such limitations on confidentiality *in advance*. The following guidelines are a good starting place. You may need to add conditions, as the example of helping a school bus driver shows.

Suggested Confidentiality Guidelines

- I recognize that my ability to provide support depends on your confidence and trust in me.
- I recognize that what you tell me is in confidence.
- I will not disclose anything you tell me to anyone without first getting your permission, unless you say that you are planning to physically harm yourself or someone else.
- I will never use the information you give me against you in any way.

The Concept of Need-to-Know

As we saw in the discussion of contextual trust, it is helpful to get to know each other. However, there are aspects of people's lives that should remain private. Where possible, confine your questioning and probing to relevant information. Encourage your peer to keep conversations focused on proactive mental health goals. Keeping communication purposeful and on topic will help maintain communication trust.

The Obligation to Disclose

Withholding pertinent information or giving false information undermines communication trust. When it comes to behavior change, slips and setbacks can feel embarrassing. Most hunches and feelings are better disclosed and are usually worth exploring. Even when information is unflattering, tell the whole truth. Explain yourself fully. Working through hunches and feelings is a good way to establish and maintain trust.

Acknowledging Misunderstandings and Mistakes

Trying something new involves a certain amount of trial and error. As you engage in peer coaching, it is highly likely that at some point you will misinterpret something, not communicate well, or be misunderstood. It is best to acknowledge such errors, apologize, explain what you have learned, and work toward new understanding. In most situations, there is little value in dwelling on mistakes, but it is important to acknowledge such errors before moving on. This builds trust and enables you to move forward with a minimum of residual baggage.

Attentive Listening

The way we listen enhances or undermines communication trust. We need to know that we are being heard and that our input is being given thoughtful consideration. You can accomplish this by looking at the person speaking, asking for clarification, and checking to see if you fully understand what is being said. Bring your focus to what is being said. Try to avoid jumping to conclusions or judging before your peer has an opportunity to fully explain and you have had a chance to digest the information. It's okay to offer your initial reactions but acknowledge that these are in fact first impressions and not well-formed conclusions. Open your mind to your peer's way of seeing things. Offer your perspective in the spirit of kindness, mutual acceptance, and the desire to be truly helpful.

Contractual Trust

Contractual trust, the third "C," is developed when peers come to agreement about how their relationship will function. This doesn't mean that rules are set in stone, but it does mean that the helping relationship will be organized in a way that respects time and other commitments. For example, it is important to establish how often to discuss the peer support goal. You may also need to consider how long you will continue to discuss the goal before you will adjust or end your conversations. Creating a schedule, sticking with it, and showing up on time are all examples of how to build contractual trust.

Contractual trust includes full disclosure of any benefits or compensation. You should explain why you are offering assistance. The reason can be as straightforward as the desire to help. If you are assisting because you have received similar help in the past, telling that story can help to build contractual trust. If you are seeking to develop skills for a future career in the helping professions, that should be disclosed. Any form of anticipated compensation should be disclosed.

Competence Trust

The final "C," competence trust, involves respecting people's knowledge, skills, abilities, and judgments. To establish this form of trust, you must be clear about your strengths and limitations. For example, you should let your peer know if you have little formal training or experience with an issue that has been raised. An offer of support should not be mistaken for a declaration that you know a great deal about your peer's goals and how they are best achieved. Frank disclosure of experience (or the lack thereof) enhances competence trust.

It is not enough to declare a lack of familiarity, knowledge, or skills. You can build trust by accompanying your peer to a library, bookstore, or other information source to get needed information. You will build competence trust by actively pursuing useful information. Reading this book is another example of how to build competence trust.

Discussing Logistics

When, where, and how to meet are important logistical considerations. You will want to come up with a plan that best fits the needs of both you and your peer.

Establishing the Format

Ideally, you and your peer will have face-to-face conversations. Such face time provides more complete communication. Facial gestures and body language communicate a lot. Your presence also says much about your high level of personal investment and engagement.

Face-to-face communication also helps us be more attentive to each other. We are less likely to multitask and more likely to listen carefully to someone in our presence. Another benefit of getting together with your peer is physical contact. A handshake and a hug bring us closer together physically and emotionally. They reinforce statements of agreement and our goodwill.

For all these reasons, the two of you should commit to at least some face-to-face conversations. Pick places that are convenient, that allow you to maintain confidentiality, that are relatively free of distracting noise and interruptions, and that are consistent with your proactive mental health goals. Private offices, a booth in an empty restaurant, a picnic table and a walking trail have all served this purpose. To establish comfort and consistency, try to stick with no more than a couple of places.

Technology brings us a multitude of additional communication formats. E-mail, phone calls, texting, and online meetings offer ways to supplement in-person conversations. These are particularly handy when travel is difficult, and time is tight. These high-tech and low-touch methods are also helpful in emergencies. There may be times when your peer needs immediate support to get through a particularly challenging day or experience. Email and snail mail can be beneficial because some people find that writing clarifies their thinking and strengthens their commitment to their goals. Sometimes the emotional distance of writing or using a phone allows for greater disclosure. You and your peer should discuss possible communication strategies.

How Often to Meet

Peer support is achieved through an ongoing conversation about personal goals. Momentum is important. Weekly discussions with breaks for holidays, illnesses and family emergencies are one good way to go. Give your discussion times the same priority normally given to work commitments. Follow-up phone calls and e-mail can supplement your weekly discussions on an as-needed basis.

Start each meeting by re-establishing your emotional connection. This balances the conversation and can be done quickly. You can share a little about your life. You may even add a ritual to the conversation such as a quick sharing of highs and lows for the week. Another example would be to exchange a favorite joke. Then you can move on to catching up on progress and to reviewing past discussions.

Also devote some time to discussing a new way to build support. For example, a conversation would begin with sharing highs and lows, followed by a review of the prior week's discussion of health behavior goals, and then turn to a discussion of how to identify and work with role models.

One advantage of peer support is that your arrangement can continue as long as your meetings are helpful.

It is useful, however, to have check-in points so that peer support conversations do not feel like an endless commitment. Two months is a good initial commitment. This will give you an opportunity to discuss most, if not all, of the six different support objectives: helping to set goals, identifying role models, eliminating barriers, locating supportive environments, working through setbacks, and celebrating success. Two months will also afford adequate time to make progress on behavior change goals. You and your peer should pick a date to discuss progress and the value of continuing to meet. At that time, you may also determine that additional conversations can be pursued through other formats, such as phone calls, texting, and email.

Checklist of Building the Foundation

Before turning to the next chapter on goal setting, use this checklist to make sure you have built a good foundation for peer support:

- We are both clear about our roles and responsibilities.
- We understand how peer support differs from other forms of helping.
- We have a plan for how often and where we will meet.
- We have identified a good end date for this round of support.
- We have agreed-upon rules for confidentiality, including when we may need to break confidentiality for outside assistance.

Worksheet for Building the Foundation

Building a solid foundation for peer support is a key to success. Answers to the following questions will help you tailor your efforts and establish high levels of trust and openness.

Questions to Ask	Commentary
1. The Right Person to Help	
Do you see me as a peer?	Find an equal and someone who has a similar frame of reference.
Can we establish a high level of trust?	Look at the potential for trust (contextual, communication, contractual and competence trust).
Do you see me as enthusiastic about your overall proactive mental health goals?	Enthusiasm generates energy and follow-through.
Do I listen well?	Listening is the most important skill in peer support.
Will it be possible to continue to discuss the proactive mental health goals?	Regular meetings for about two months help maintain momentum.

2. Building Trust and Openness	
How will we really get to know each other?	Personal connection establishes contextual trust.
Do we have good communication?	Open and honest communication makes the relationship more powerful.
What are the limits of confidentiality?	Decide what rare situations would require breaking confidence (such as a situation in which physical harm or criminal activity is being contemplated).
Do you understand why I am offering support?	Full disclosure of all the reasons for helping builds contractual trust.
What skill and experience, if any, do we have going into this?	To develop competence trust, get clear about your skills, or lack thereof.
3. Setting Peer Support Logistics	
When and where should we meet?	Decide on a place that is relatively private, convenient, and comfortable.
What format will we use to communicate?	Decide about in-person, phone calls, text, and e-mail communication and any times when communication should be limited (such as not calling after 7:00 p.m.).

Do I have time for this or am I overcommitted?	A peer support relationship requires thoughtful attention.
What date should we set for completing the first round of support?	Decide on a date so that your conversations don't feel like an open-ended commitment. Then check in to determine if additional support is desirable.

Chapter 3
Setting Proactive Mental Health Goals

A goal without a plan is just a wish.

—Antoine de Saint-Exupéry

Better Together is about supporting a family member, friend, or coworker in their efforts to prevent mental illness and achieve optimal well-being. When picking goals and strategies it is often helpful to begin with a variety of choices. Proactive mental health is an overlapping matrix of six building blocks of behaviors and attitudes that prevent mental illness and increase overall mental well-being. These factors are the wellness ingredients that create mental and emotional quality of life. Together, they prevent and heal mental illness.

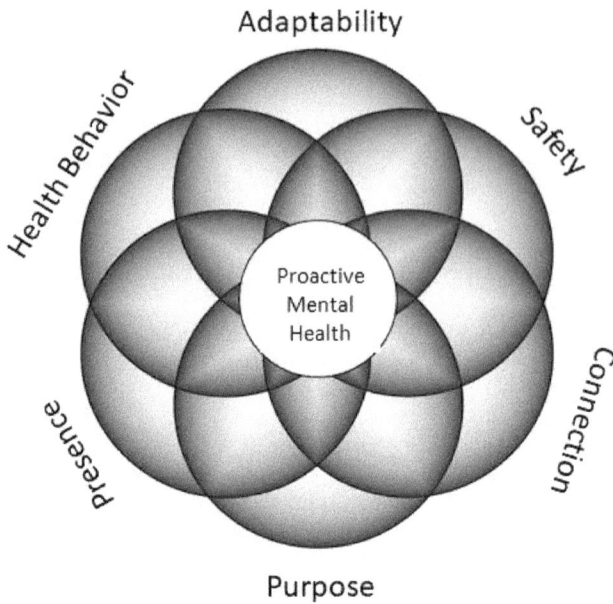

Almost everyone already has proactive mental health strengths. Most people also have at least one attitude or behavior that could be improved. Help your peer to consider the full scope of attitudes and behaviors that promote emotional well-being. The proactive mental health self-assessment provides a way to see how we are doing. You and your peer can discuss the results. Reactions to the self-assessment results can stimulate a conversation about setting proactive mental health goals.

Proactive Mental Health Self-Assessment

Proactive mental health is a constellation of behaviors and attitudes that prevent mental illness and increase overall mental well-being. The following self-assessment asks about 26 current practices. Your answers will help prioritize efforts to support mental health.

Instructions: *Using the five-point scale, rate how consistently you experience the proactive mental health attitudes and behaviors.*

5 Always

4 Often

3 Sometimes

2 Rarely

1 Never

NA Not applicable

How are you doing this week?

ATTITUDES AND BEHAVIORS	Current Practice
Presence	
Are you able to focus on the here and now?	5 4 3 2 1 NA
Do you declutter and destress your life so you can experience inner peace?	5 4 3 2 1 NA
Do you practice daily stress management techniques such as taking a walk, meditation, or yoga?	5 4 3 2 1 NA

How are you doing this week?

ATTITUDES AND BEHAVIORS	Current Practice
Connection	
Are you able to love and be loved?	5 4 3 2 1 NA
Do you spend time with friends most days?	5 4 3 2 1 NA
Can you forgive?	5 4 3 2 1 NA
Are you grateful?	5 4 3 2 1 NA
Can you trust others, and are you trustworthy?	5 4 3 2 1 NA
Are you good at teamwork?	5 4 3 2 1 NA
Adaptability	
Can you handle disappointment?	5 4 3 2 1 NA
Do you persist in the face of challenges?	5 4 3 2 1 NA
Are you open to trying new ways of doing things?	5 4 3 2 1 NA
Do you consider your strengths before taking on tasks and challenges?	5 4 3 2 1 NA
Do you avoid seeing problems or bad news as permanent, pervasive (affecting all things), or personal (about you)?	5 4 3 2 1 NA
Purpose	
Do you feel like you are making a difference?	5 4 3 2 1 NA
Do you regularly do things that give your life meaning?	5 4 3 2 1 NA

ATTITUDES AND BEHAVIORS	Current Practice
Do you experience passion and commitment?	5 4 3 2 1 NA
Safety	
Do you feel economically secure?	5 4 3 2 1 NA
Are you free from physical and emotional violence and abuse?	5 4 3 2 1 NA
Do you live, work, and play in healthy physical environments?	5 4 3 2 1 NA
Health Behavior	
Are you current on your preventive medical health screenings?	5 4 3 2 1 NA
Do you get help with mental and physical health problems early on?	5 4 3 2 1 NA
Do you eat a healthy diet?	5 4 3 2 1 NA
Do you drink alcohol or use recreational drugs moderately, if at all?	5 4 3 2 1 NA
Do you get adequate rest?	5 4 3 2 1 NA
Do you take part in 30 minutes of physical activity most days of the week?	5 4 3 2 1 NA

Review the responses. How is your peer doing with proactive mental health? A person can be mentally healthy without achieving all 26 practices. Here are five recommendations for follow-up discussions:

- **Review strengths.** These would be those questions with scores of four or five. Acknowledging those aspects of proactive mental health that are already in place is a good place to start. Explore those positive qualities with your peer. How can they be used to address any remaining opportunities for improvement? Explore how they developed their lifestyle strengths. See if there's something to learn from past successes. Build upon these strengths when approaching issues that still need attention. Proactive mental health strengths are important because they indicate your peer's past success and are the building blocks for future progress.

- **Review those areas that need attention.** These would be questions with scores of one, two, or three. It's okay if your peer's answers indicate they do not practice a proactive mental health behavior and yet are satisfied with the way things stand. Look instead at the areas where there are both a need and a desire for change. Try not to impose your own opinion, but instead ask questions to get clarification about their priorities.

- **Examine any goals not covered in the assessment.** Determine whether all interests were adequately covered and discuss any gaps or variations that better reflect your peer's personal interests.

- **Explore possible connections between goals.** Proactive mental health goals often address several behaviors that overlap in such a way that one goal spills over into other goals. Proactive mental health is an integrative process that engages the mind, body, and spirit. By examining possible links among goals, you may come up with new practices that address many goals simultaneously. For example, a daily yoga practice could address goals for physical activity and for presence. Similarly, someone seeking to lower stress may find that sleep, exercise, nutrition, and increased social engagement are helpful. Consider prioritizing changes that accomplish multiple goals.

- **Examine personal passion, motivation, and enthusiasm for the goals.** These goals need to be important enough to inspire continued commitment. Enthusiasm and drive make changes easier to maintain and more enjoyable. The best goals are not always the easiest or most accessible. Attitude may trump convenience.

Exploring Benefits

With your peer, explore the purposes of achieving their goals. Your conversation may reveal additional benefits of proactive mental health. Achieving proactive mental health goals can deliver multiple benefits. For example, in addition to self-preservation, some people pursue proactive mental health so we can be better role models for our children or grandchildren.

One way to gain clarity on a goal is to determine the potential benefits. The following four questions can be a conversation starter:

- **Is this goal aimed at managing an illness and restoring vitality?** A heart attack survivor may pursue mental well-being to reduce the likelihood of another attack.

- **Will the goal improve quality of life?** A workaholic may take a sabbatical from work to reset a healthy work/life balance.

- **Is the goal directed at avoiding future mental illness?** Although mental illness is common, individuals can lower their risk.

- **Is this goal aimed at peak performance?** An athlete may adopt a yoga routine to improve their ability to compete. An artist may go for a morning walk to enhance their creative energy.

Help Set Shorter-Term and Longer-Term Goals

Although the big goal is the focus of your peer's efforts, it is also helpful to have smaller goals so you can celebrate successes along the way. A goal of economic security, for example, might involve a year or more of saving money. Part of this goal may be taking steps toward a more financially rewarding job. Immediate actions may also be within reach, such as cutting costs on monthly subscriptions.

Access Available Research

It is often worthwhile to investigate what experts say are reasonable goals. Mental health professionals, books, journals, and a respected website can be helpful in determining goals.

Find Your Peer's Place on the Road Map of Change

Most behavior change goals are achieved in stages. The process often begins with developing a commitment to change and ends with having a change so firmly in place that setbacks are no longer likely. Many of us are somewhere in the middle of this process. Work with your peer to identify their current stage of change. Such a conversation will make it easier to focus on the most meaningful steps to take now.

Sometimes the personal change process is not clear. Added clarity helps break complex changes into achievable actions. It also increases accountability. James Prochaska and Carlo DiClemente created a useful behavior change roadmap that is incorporated into the following table. Talk with your peer to help identify where they are and to set the short-term and long-term goals that are most meaningful now.

Using the five-point scale, rate your level agreement with the following statements

A Roadmap for Personal Change

	Stage of Change	Appropriate Change Goal
1.	**DEVELOPING COMMITMENT:** Your peer is not truly convinced about the importance of the goal. Your peer may be just exploring the general possibility of taking on a goal. For example, someone might have told them the goal is worthwhile.	If you find yourselves in the "exploratory phase," then the goal is to get more information about the value of such a change.
2.	**CONTEMPLATION:** Your peer would like to change and thinks they are likely to attempt change in the next six months.	Your peer should set a date for making the change. Engaging in conversation about the possibilities can often help solidify their thinking.

3.	**PREPARATION:** Your peer is planning to act in the immediate future (usually within the next month) and is determining the best strategy to carry out the change.	Together, develop the plan for how the change will be carried out. To build accountability, your peer could let others know about the intention to change.
4.	**ACTION:** Your peer is actively engaged in making changes.	Help your peer adjust to the new lifestyle and manage challenges as they emerge.
5.	**MAINTENANCE:** Your peer is working to integrate the behavior change into her normal day-to-day life.	Continue to pay attention to the behavior and work through any relapse. The central focus for your peer is to get comfortable with the new behavior and have it become fully integrated into other aspects of life. Your peer can also mentor someone with similar goals. Teaching tends to reinforce positive changes.

| 6. | **MOVING ON:** Your peer has maintained the change for a year or more and is no longer tempted by the old behavior. | Help your peer set new goals. Move on from support systems that are focused exclusively on the prior goal. It is no longer useful for your peer to look at himself as one step from relapse. It's time to move on to other goals and interests. |

These stages of change are not a fixed or necessary process. Sometimes people just put their mind to something and the change clicks into place. However, discussing the stages can be very useful in setting both current, intermediate, and long-term goals. This model can also help determine the most appropriate support. For instance, if someone is already making change, a conversation about why to change may not be well received or necessary. The decision as has already been made.

Clarifying Goals

It is likely that your peer has several goals in mind. The following questions help clarify and prioritize these goals.

- **If there is more than one goal, what are the top priorities?** Have a conversation about current proactive mental health goals, including how much change should be taken on now, and whether some goals should be addressed later. Everyone has limits. A change must be important enough to maintain interest and engagement. Goals must be big enough to be challenging but not so big that they feel overwhelming.

- **Do you both have the necessary information to set good goals?** It is important to separate facts from fiction. Try to find trustworthy information. Is the information supported by adequate research? Does the source have a reputation for accuracy, or is the information part of a sales pitch? Has the information held up over time and with repeated investigation? Is the information appropriate in terms of matching up with your peer's age, gender, and other characteristics? You and you peer may need to investigate reputable websites, go to a library, or consult health experts to get additional input about the appropriate behavioral goals and how they should be achieved.

- **Do you have good ways to measure progress?** Ideally, there will be markers that allow you to regularly assess goal achievement. Measurement should have a behavioral component. For example, the goal for financial security might be to pay off credit card debt. Additional measures of progress should be explored. For example, your peer could set a retirement savings goal to maximize an employer's matching contribution. Concrete numbers can tell your peer how they're doing.

Embracing the Proactive Mental Health Journey

Proactive mental health is a process of continual growth. Goals evolve as competing priorities are in flux. Sometimes goals change because people gain new insights. Such change could be the result of personal experience. Sometimes goals change because the social influences have changed. Peers help track and witness this evolution. Notetaking and a review can be particularly useful forms of peer support when someone seems scattered or lacks follow-through on important decisions.

However, in the final analysis, we need to embrace learning and growth by allowing for the natural evolution of goals. Mental health is a journey. The goal posts often change. Empower your peer by embracing their journey.

Goal-Setting Checklist

Before turning to the next chapter on identifying role models, summarize your goal-setting findings. The following checklist will help you determine whether you have covered the key ideas:

- We examined the underlying purpose of the proactive mental health goals. We have determined whether the goals are directed at (1) managing an illness, (2) lowering the risk of future health problems, (3) improving quality of life, or (4) achieving peak performance

- We examined the overall proactive mental health picture to reveal a range of goals. We determined how some goals could be accomplished together. We prioritized the goals to determine which goal should be tackled first.

- We investigated the facts pertaining to the proactive mental health goals. We identified the best sources of information available for setting specific, measurable, short-term, and long-term goals. Our goals are informed by the best available science and research. The approaches we are taking have shown their worth in situations like ours.

- We discussed the six stages of behavior change. We have benchmarks for moving along the stages toward our proactive mental health goal(s).

Worksheet for Setting Proactive Mental Health Goals

Goal setting often involves several underlying decisions. Answers to the following questions will help you tailor your efforts and establish a clearer understanding of your peer's goals.

1. Embracing the Proactive mental health Journey

What are the main purposes for achieving the goal?	Proactive mental health goals are often associated with addressing an existing illness, preventing future illness, improving overall quality of life, achieving peak performance, or some combination of these.
What is the social context for achieving the goal?	Sometimes proactive mental health goals are set to please others, to fit in, to be more desirable, to be caring of others and to be more responsible.
What are the behavior change goals?	Identify goals across the spectrum of the six proactive mental health dimensions.
What are current behavioral strengths?	Identify strengths associated with proactive mental health.
Are there ways that current strengths can be applied to new proactive mental health goals?	Strengths encourage forward movement.

Are there some actions that will address two or more behavior change priorities?	Many proactive mental health activities, such as yoga and physical activity, have several payoffs.
What proactive mental health goals is my peer passionate about?	Goal achievement usually requires energy and passion.
2. Clarifying Goals	
If there is more than one goal, what are the top priorities?	Review the findings of the previous questions to identify priorities.
What information is needed to set a good goal?	Proactive mental health goals such as improving diet and exercise often lead to recommendations for short- and long-term goals, as well as strategies for achieving those goals.
How will we measure progress?	It is easier to see progress when goals are clear, specific, and measurable. Such feedback keeps goals on track.
3. Working the Change Process	
What is the current stage of change?	Knowing the stage facilitates focusing on the tasks that are most meaningful.
What will indicate forward movement to another stage of change?	The stages form mini-goals and a road map for seeing progress as the behavior change unfolds.

Chapter 4
Identifying Role Models

I'm not a role model...Just because I dunk a basketball doesn't mean I should raise your kids.

—Charles Barkley

What makes a good role model? A role model doesn't have to be in a position of high visibility or influence. Instead, a good role model is someone who has achieved a desired outcome under relatable circumstances. Such a role model can be found among coworkers, friends, family members, or the community at large.

Identifying role models is a key part of our model of proactive mental health because these people can offer a window into a successful future. Why wait to see the benefits of change when others have already achieved the same or similar goals? Why not look at what has worked? Why not avoid some of the common mistakes and pitfalls? When it comes to proactive mental health goals, there's no need to re-invent the wheel. Why not get encouragement from someone who has walked in the same shoes? Visualizing success through a role model can accelerate progress.

You may be relieved to know that you are not expected to be your peer's role model. You don't have to have achieved the same or similar proactive mental health goals. Instead, you can work with your peer to seek out one or more role models. You can help your peer take full advantage of a role model's experiences.

Exchanging Success Stories

A good way to begin the conversation about finding a good role model is to relate the task to your own experiences. Most of us have experiences that make us role models for some sort of behavior change. It is likely that your stories include successes that will inspire others. Think about goals you have achieved and obstacles you have had to overcome. Your peer is also likely to have achieved some successes. Exchange stories of times in your lives when you have achieved proactive mental health goals.

Ask:

- What was your proactive mental health goal?
- What were the reasons you made the change?
- What strategies worked?
- What challenges did you overcome?
- How did other people help?

These are the same questions that might be asked of a future role model. You will be looking for someone with the capacity to answer such questions as they relate specifically to your peer's proactive mental health goal.

Finding Role Models

Begin the search for people who have achieved your peer's proactive mental health goal. Don't be discouraged if finding good role models requires some digging. These are sometimes private stories, and it is frequently considered bragging to openly discuss successes. Although a couple of candidates could be enough, try to brainstorm and track down a larger list of candidates before settling upon your final choices. The following strategies are good ways to start:

- Look among family, coworkers, friends, and acquaintances. Think about the various groups you belong to. Has anyone mentioned a similar proactive mental health goal? These people are often open to a face-to-face discussion as well as follow-up support.

- Ask family, coworkers, and friends if they know someone who has achieved a similar proactive mental health goal. There may be a suitable role model among these contacts. A friend of a friend is often open to helping.

- Find a local course or support group that focuses on your goal. The teacher or recent course graduates make knowledgeable role models. Many people continue to attend support group meetings well after they have achieved their goals. These people are often enthusiastic about helping and sharing their knowledge.

- A company wellness program coordinator or employee assistance program counselor may suggest some candidates who are willing to be contacted. Some helping professionals keep an active list of such role models.

- Chat rooms and discussion groups are common online. You can find conversations that focus on proactive mental health goals. The participants in these discussions can be helpful role models.

- Blogs are another source of support online. A search on a proactive mental health goal may turn up one or more blogs that document the personal stories of potential role models.

- Associations have programs dedicated to proactive mental health goals. Many of these groups are organized to address a particular disease. The local chapters and the national organization can help identify role model candidates, suggest online and in-person resources, offer support groups, and provide literature with success stories.

- Self-help books, online videos, and movies feature proactive mental health success stories. Libraries, bookstores, and YouTube are good sources. Many books in medical and self-help categories include personal testimonials. The authors frequently relate their own experiences to illustrate key concepts. Online videos are available on most proactive mental health topics and feature eligible role models telling their stories in a compelling and entertaining format. The main disadvantage of these role models is that it is unlikely that you will be able to establish an ongoing conversation with them. Some sources, however, will reference web-sites that support conversations with the author or with other readers.

Sizing Up Role Models

An effective role model provides inspiration, insight, encouragement, and an appreciation of the many benefits of successful change. The following table describes key qualities to seek out and those to avoid in a role model.

Picking Effective Role Models

Qualities of an Effective Role Model	Qualities of an Ineffective Role Model
Has achieved similar goals under similar circumstances.	Has achieved a goal that differs in important ways. For example, a new parent who is seeking to get a good night's sleep is substantially different from an elder seeking to sleep through the night.
Recognizes that great benefits were realized through successful lifestyle change.	Views the change efforts as more trouble than they were worth.
Is willing to share their story, including the difficult parts.	Shares nothing about personal experience beyond that it was successful.
Is willing to take time to provide personal background information and to establish trust.	Is not able or willing to share personal background information or build trust.
Sees change as a process.	Expects quick fixes.
Is not quick to criticize or to judge.	Immediately makes character judgments.

Believes it is important to get support from others and shares how other people played a role in the their success.	Thinks change is best achieved without the support or involvement of others.
Acknowledges that change can be a challenge.	Says that change is easy.
Gives others permission to create their own path to success.	Recognizes only one way to success: "my way."

Use this table of role model qualities to help your peer narrow down a list of possible role models to the best candidates. The table may also be helpful in conversations with a new role model. Sharing some of the qualities listed in the table will help clarify the type of support your peer is seeking. The qualities may also be useful later. Your peer can use the list to probe deeper for the challenges the role model experienced in achieving their goal. The list can also help determine whether your peer has gotten the full benefit of their relationship with a role model.

Connecting with a Role Model

You may want to help your peer think through the best way to approach a potential role model. Asking someone to be a role model can be a tricky proposition. The term "role model" sometimes implies a level of perfection, and many people don't see themselves in this way. A good approach is for your peer to explain their proactive mental health goal and to ask a role model candidate if they achieved something similar. Follow-up questions could flesh out the role model's experience. At the end of the initial conversation, ask if it is okay to ask follow-up questions as efforts progress.

Questions for a Role Model

Have a set of questions ready before meeting with a potential role model. This will provide the most useful information and help keep the conversation flowing. The following questions are a good place to begin:

- What did you accomplish?
- What strategies did you use?
- How did you track your progress?
- What were some of the benefits of making the changes?
- What was particularly difficult, and how did you overcome those challenges?
- What help did you get from others?
- Who inspired you or served as your role model?
- What sources of good information did you find?
- Can I check in with you after I begin to make changes?

Whenever possible, your peer should try to meet face-to-face with a role model. The in-person experience increases the level of communication, allows for personal warmth, and enhances believability. Set aside adequate time so the conversation will not be rushed. Forty-five minutes to an hour usually works best.

Checklist for Identifying Role Models

Role models can offer immense inspiration. They can be a beacon, a light at the end of the tunnel, as your peer embarks on a lifestyle change. This means that it's well worth looking beyond immediate friends and family to find the best possible people to fill this role. The following checklist will help you and your peer determine whether you have addressed the potential for working with role models:

- We brainstormed sources of role model candidates and determined how to get their contact information and follow up.

- We discussed role model qualities to get a clear picture of the desired characteristics.

- We contacted candidates and began the conversation with them.

- We followed up with role models with in-person meetings and progress reports.

Worksheet for Identifying Role Models

Finding a good role model involves several decisions. Answers to the following questions will help you tailor your efforts to your peer's needs and preferences.

Questions to Ask	Commentary
1. Comfort with Reaching Out and Self-disclosure	
Identifying and talking with role models may reveal personal information. How do you feel about this? Are there strategies and guidelines we need to adopt to limit such personal disclosure?	There are potential role models that can be contacted discreetly or without the need to disclose your peer's goals. Finding a role model online or in a book are examples. However, if privacy is not a concern, face-to-face conversations tend to be most beneficial.
2. Sizing Up Role Models	
What qualities are you looking for in an ideal role model?	Review the list of qualities of an effective role model and visualize the qualities desired.
What are the selection criteria for prioritizing the list of potential role models?	The criteria may help eliminate some candidates and help determine the most likely candidates.

3. Finding Role Models	
Who are the potential role model candidates?	Identify as many highly qualified and willing individuals as possible.
4. Connecting with Role Models	
What is the plan for contacting potential role models?	Be sure to approach candidates in a friendly way that invites their assistance.
What questions do we have for the role model?	Organize the interview in such a way that the role models will have an opportunity to share their stories and make useful suggestions.
What can we do to enable follow-up conversations?	Questions and tasks change throughout the behavior change process. Leave the door open for additional input from role models.

Chapter 5

Eliminating Barriers to Change

It's part of life to have obstacles. It's about overcoming obstacles; that's the key to happiness.

—HERBIE HANCOCK

ONE OF THE greatest proactive mental health stories of all time took place on Robin Island just off the coast of Cape Town, South Africa. This was the site of a political prison that held Nelson Mandela and other South African leaders for several decades. The prisoners were held in small cells and allowed few privileges. Mandela and the other prisoners recognized that they would need their health if they were to survive and continue their work to end apartheid, so they committed themselves to doing everything within their power to sustain their mental and physical fitness. They exercised in their cramped cells and tried to eat as well as they could. They formed an underground school to sharpen their thinking and to sustain their mental health and well-being.

These South African leaders endured prison life for several decades, By the time of their final release in 1990, the prisoners' discipline and creativity were so inspirational that even their once-cruel prison guards had been moved to feel admiration and friendship for their charges.

Their story illustrates that one can pursue well-being even under the most oppressive conditions. Fortunately, few of us will ever endure the hardships experienced by Mandela and his fellow prisoners. Most of us experience barriers to proactive mental health that are more of an inconvenience than a true hardship. However, the psychological and physical barriers we experience are real.

We often find that we lack the time, equipment, and other resources needed to achieve proactive mental health goals. We often find it difficult to justify our healthy activities. And many of us lack the discipline and focus to stick with a plan of action. Your peer undoubtedly has some barriers in the way. Your peer needs your help to adequately address those barriers. You can help find ways over and around barriers to behavior change.

Resource Needs to Achieve Proactive Mental Health Goals

Resources are often needed to make the healthy choice the easy choice. The following table lists the most common resource needs and explains how such resources can reduce barriers to success.

Resource Needs	Discussion
Time	Time is an important ingredient of success. Estimate how much time your peer might need to achieve the proactive mental health goal. For example, if physical activity is the goal, how much time will be spent exercising? Another aspect of time is making the new behavior a regular or routine part of the day. Help your peer find a time when the needed energy levels and equipment are available, and a time when other commitments will not compete.
Support	We all juggle our responsibilities and commitments with others. Ideally, coworkers, supervisors, housemates, and family will accommodate any shifts in responsibility needed to support your peer's proactive mental health goals. Determine who should be consulted and how to approach them. Determine how responsibilities such as childcare will be covered. If such accommodation is not available, how can these barriers be overcome or worked around?

Equipment	Proactive mental health activities require the right tools. For example, yoga routines benefit from having comfortable clothes, a yoga mat, and a quiet space. In a similar way, a good garden plot and access to a health-oriented grocery store may be important when your peer's goal is to achieve a healthy diet. Determine any equipment that will be needed and how it will be found.
Expertise	Behavior change frequently requires know-how. It will be much easier for your peer to stick with a behavior that they are good at and feel confident about. Formal training, mentoring and self-study can build knowledge, skill, and confidence levels. Together, determine the best way to secure the information, practice, and skills your peer needs for success.

Focus	Mental health and a positive attitude are important factors in sustaining behavior change. For example, sleep is essential to a healthy attention span and to thinking processes. Anxiety can undermine your peer's focus. Mood also plays a role in achieving proactive mental health goals. Fortunately, many goals, such as exercise and healthy eating, enhance psychological well-being. Determine how any unmet emotional and psychological needs may pose barriers. Plan for addressing those needs.

Conducting a Strengths Review

Our strengths, not our weaknesses, help us move forward. Barriers can feel overwhelming when we lose sight of our strengths. You can help your peer regain forward momentum by conducting a strengths review. Review resource needs and ask your peer the following questions:

- **What resources are already available for achieving your goal?** Think about strengths in terms of time, support, equipment, expertise, and focus. Come up with a comprehensive list.

- **How can strengths be applied toward acquiring additional resources?** For example, your peer may have enthusiastic friends (a strength) willing to care for her children while they go for a daily run.

Breaking Down Barriers

If requests don't work, some obstacles to proactive mental health must be confronted head-on. If social pressures and a lack of resources are standing in the way of proactive mental health, then it is not only appropriate, but also just, to demand that those barriers change. A society is in trouble when someone must be a hero or a martyr to do what's right.

Many support systems for proactive mental health behavior are unfunded and under-resourced. For example, if there is no quiet place for contemplation or meditation, people can join together to advocate for such a space to be created. You can work with your peer to enable change. Here's how:

- Discuss why proactive mental health is a human right. All people deserve good health and an opportunity to achieve their potential. People should be encouraged to pursue proactive mental health goals, not discouraged. For example, the lack of healthy restaurants or supermarkets and affordable fitness facilities undercuts proactive mental health. Working long hours or forgoing vacations, which is often seen as necessary to "get ahead" or "succeed," also undermines proactive mental health. Explore conditions that undermine growth, especially those related to your peer's goal. Discuss the role of society and social institutions in fostering proactive mental health. Consider whether appropriate requests can be made of the workplace or community. Although changes may take a while, you will be paving the way for others who follow you.

- Develop strategies for working with "gatekeepers," such as a supervisor, coworker, or housemate. Asking for support frequently requires a game plan. For example, a work supervisor is more likely to extend the lunch hour to accommodate fitness if (1) the request is made respectfully, (2) the work still gets done, and (3) the supervisor understands the relationship between health and productivity. With your peer, take turns role-playing such gatekeeper conversations.

- Discuss how to break down barriers to proactive mental health. Work rules and conditions, government service, laws and the activities of community groups can all support proactive mental health. There is some truth to the saying "the squeaky wheel gets the grease." Join with others to ask for needed changes within your organization or community.

Coping with Barriers

Favorable conditions facilitate positive behavior change. But as the Robin Island inmates demonstrated, proactive mental health can be achieved even in the face of adversity. The following coping strategies may help your peer move through some barriers that resist change. Advise your peer to:

- **Join with others.** You do not have to do this alone. As we will see in the chapter on locating supportive environments, support groups offer their members tremendous psychological strength and hope and encouragement.

- **Consult role models.** These people have likely experienced adversity and devised good coping strategies. Ask for their ideas and encouragement. See Chapter 3 for more on role models.

- **Change your focus.** A barrier does not negate the benefits of other available resources. Focus on what you want, your strengths and resources, and what can be accomplished. Make it a practice to review strengths and celebrate progress. Positive thoughts can make a struggle less taxing.

- **Be kind in other aspects of life.** Where possible, cut back on other responsibilities. Increase the number of pleasurable activities in your day. Allow for renewal activities such as sleep, exercise and socializing with supportive friends.

- **Use any barriers to mobilize determination.** Barriers, especially when they are unkind, unjust, or arbitrary, can spawn outrage and resistance. Take a stand and resist. Don't let injustice and thoughtlessness win.

Checklist for Eliminating Barriers

Barriers can make proactive mental health goals much more challenging to achieve. Addressing barriers requires creativity and good problem-solving skills. Your peer is much more likely to come up with good strategies when the two of you approach resource needs together. The following checklist will help organize your efforts:

- We have a clear picture of the resources (time, support, equipment, expertise, and focus) that are needed to achieve proactive mental health goals, and we know of any gaps in resources.

- We have reviewed existing resource strengths and how these may be applied to address barriers to change.

- We have requested or demanded needed resources.

- Where needed, we have engaged the support of gatekeepers such as supervisors, family members and housemates.

- Where needed, we have brought down barriers by effectively advocating for change.

- We have developed coping strategies for moving forward despite remaining barriers.

Worksheet for Eliminating Barriers to Change

Answers to the following questions will help you tailor your efforts to support your peer's efforts to find resources and lower the barriers to change.

Questions to Ask	Commentary
1. Determining Needs	
How much time is needed, and where should it fit in the schedule?	Although proactive mental health goals for eliminating negative behavior may free up time, many positive practices, such as physical activity, require time for the new behavior. Ideally, this would be a predictable and regular time that allows for a routine.
What backing or permission would help?	Some goals require that your peer to get a release of responsibilities from other tasks such as work or childcare. Permission and cooperation can help them succeed.
What equipment would help?	Some goals are best achieved with tools, clothes, specific foods, and other physical resources.

What expertise would help?	Proper instructions and training can make behavior change easier.
What mental health and attitude issues need to be addressed?	Lack of sleep, psychiatric conditions, anxiety, and other mental factors can interfere with change. In contrast, a positive attitude and overall mental health make it more likely that your peer's goals can be maintained.
2. Conducting a Strengths Review	
What resources are already available?	Take stock of existing resources, as such resources form a base upon which to work.
How can available resources be applied toward getting needed resources?	The people and places that already serve as resources are likely to offer clues about filling remaining gaps in your peer's resources.

3. Breaking Down Barriers	
What is the justification for asking for resources to achieve the proactive mental health goal?	Confidence that the goal is a good one and that it is worthy of needed resources is important to making the case for more resources.
Who will need to cooperate and how shall they be approached?	A strategy helps in asking for resources from gatekeepers such as supervisors and family members
How can we eliminate or reduce barriers?	Sometimes it is necessary to petition for changes in rules, lack of resources and other barriers. Such advocacy can be done solo or by joining with others.
4. Coping with Barriers	
What coping strategies will be used where resources are unavailable, and barriers remain?	It is unlikely that change will occur under perfect conditions. Help your peer recognize the barriers and develop workarounds or coping strategies.

Chapter 6

Locating Supportive Environments

Be true to yourself and surround yourself with positive, supportive people.

—PAYAL KADAKIA

WHAT COMES TO mind when you think of a supportive environment? Perhaps you visualize a tropical paradise or a gathering of smiling friends. A supportive environment does include special occasions and interesting places, but for our purposes right now, we're looking for something far less exotic. We're focusing on supportive influences in the daily environment, like the people and the places in your peer's daily routine.

Home, the workplace, the neighborhood, and the grocery store are just some of the settings that influence behavior. In a similar way, housemates, spouses, friends, children, coworkers, teammates, club members and neighbors form our immediate social – and hopefully supportive – circles.

Helping your peer find and create physical, emotional,

and social environments that support their proactive mental health goals is an important peer support strategy. In this chapter we discuss how you can bring environmental influences into focus, and how to modify these influences so that they better support your peer's desired proactive mental health behavior. The perspectives of anthropologists, architects, and city planners shed light on how to understand and create supportive environments.

Finding and Creating Supportive Physical Environments

When an architect plans a house, each room is designed to support its function. In a similar way, a behavior is easier to achieve with a supportive physical environment. For example, if physical safety is the goal, living and working in a safe and friendly neighborhood is crucial.

You can help your peer find supportive places, limit exposure to unsupportive environments, and change those aspects of environments that work against proactive mental health. Together, think about where your peer will be carrying out the activities associated with their goal. Is it:

- Safe?
- Convenient?
- Well-maintained?
- A pleasant temperature?
- Appropriately equipped?
- Affordable?
- Comfortable?

Keep an eye out for unsupportive factors – the opposite of the previous list. For example, although I enjoy going to a yoga class, getting there (driving and parking) is a pain. I'm better off going once a week with friends and taking online classes at home the rest of the week.

What is necessary to make the physical environment more supportive of the proactive mental health goal? Having assessed the physical environment, you and your peer can plan how to change recreational, work and living spaces so that they are more supportive. Consider finding new places. For example, early spring and late fall in Vermont are not conducive to outdoor exercise. A lucky few travel out of state, but many migrate to health clubs and indoor skating rinks. We also set up treadmills and exercise bikes in our homes. The following questions are useful for pursuing supportive physical environments:

- What places support your proactive mental health goals, and how can you spend more time in these places?

- What places are unsupportive, and how can they be changed or avoided?

- How can you find or create new supportive places?

Mobilizing Proactive Mental Health Buddies

Many people find it easier and more enjoyable to do things with a companion. A proactive mental health buddy is someone who has the same or a very similar goal. A proactive mental health buddy may also be engaged in peer support conversations, but this is not a requirement. You can help your peer find one or more proactive mental health buddies.

The power of the buddy approach has worked wonders in my own life. Two days a week, I get together with a couple of friends at 6 a.m. to jog. On Sunday mornings, I do my "long run" with a running club. During these jogs, we talk about current events, our lives and our exercise goals. These times with my buddies are among my best. They keep me energized even though I'm not usually an early riser. My buddies make my fitness routine truly enjoyable. We are in this together.

Consider the following questions when helping your peer establish proactive mental health buddy relationships.

- **Do your peer's proactive mental health goals lend themselves to partnering with another person?** Think creatively about this. Even activities that are generally done alone, such as financial planning or managing an illness, could be done more easily with another person who is pursing similar goals.

- **Who would make the best proactive mental health buddies?** Existing social networks often offer good choices for buddies. For example, if your peer is trying to eat healthier, they could partner with housemates. Frequent contact and a shared refrigerator enhance the benefit. In addition to existing social networks, buddies can be found in a support group, at a seminar or online. Use the same approaches recommended in the "Identifying Role Models" chapter.

- **What are barriers to finding proactive mental health buddies?** In American culture there is a myth that the things we do by ourselves are somehow more enduring than and superior to what we do with others. This has been a particularly strong message to men. Encourage your peer to reach out to others. Once the ice is broken, people usually find that the buddy approach is far more enjoyable and sustainable than the go-it-alone approach.

- **What is the ideal schedule for connecting with proactive mental health buddies?** This depends on the goal. If the goal involves a routine, buddies can do that routine together. Weekly contact helps keeps the energy flowing. I joined Weight Watchers with my wife and neighbors. We attended weekly meetings together and then went out for sushi afterward to celebrate our progress.

Finding and Creating Supportive Cultural Environments

How would anthropologists rate someone's chances of achieving a proactive mental health goal? They would look at the influence of tools, buildings, and social networks. They would look to see if proactive mental health behaviors are rewarded. They might also examine rites of passage, rituals, and symbols – do they detract from or enhance pro-active mental health? Just like an anthropologist, you and your peer can examine cultural environments to plan how to avoid unsupportive environments in favor of supportive cultural forces.

Some unhealthy aspects of our current cultures are obvious. Such is the case with the excesses of a caffeine-drinking culture. American culture's epidemic of overeating is another example of a readily apparent health problem.

When addressing cultural support, you and your peer will also want to look for more subtle influences. There are three powerful, but too often overlooked, cultural dimensions: cultural climate, cultural norms, and cultural policies and procedures, which I refer to as touch points.

Fostering a Supportive Cultural Climate

When people don't get along, it is difficult to focus on personal growth. In a hostile environment, people are angry, frustrated, and uncooperative. In the United States, airports have come to symbolize such settings. The buzz is predominantly negative and filled with suspicion. High security, overbooked flights and disgruntled passengers and airline employees keep people on edge. Other common examples of hostile or highly stressful environments are companies undergoing downsizing and families going through a divorce. Help your peer toward either resolving such conflict or finding ways to avoid the daily grind of unpleasantness.

A good climate takes different forms in households, workplaces, and neighborhoods. Personal change is much easier to pursue in a friendly and cohesive social environment. In a relationship, this might be referred to as the honeymoon phase. On a worksite, it's called great teamwork. A strong sense of community, a shared vision and a positive outlook are dimensions of a supportive climate. These factors enhance individual and organizational growth. A sense of community provides for trust and openness. A shared vision enables people to be inspired by a common direction. A positive outlook makes it possible to use individual and collective strengths in meeting challenges. Finding or creating a healthy climate is a useful lifestyle change skill.

Your peer can examine the climate with the Cultural Climate Test. The questions examine the three climatic dimensions.

Cultural Climate Test

Instructions: Focus on one social group or setting at a time. You can repeat the test for the important social groups in your life, such as your household, work group, family, and community organization. Rate your level of agreement with the following statements on the 5-point scale: (5) strongly agree, (4) agree, (3) undecided/don't know, (2) disagree, and (1) strongly disagree.

	Sense of Community
5 4 3 2 1	I know the people in my group really well.
5 4 3 2 1	I feel as if I belong here.
5 4 3 2 1	Members would support or care for me in a time of need.
5 4 3 2 1	I trust these people.

5 4 3 2 1	I feel comfortable saying what's on my mind.
	Shared Vision
5 4 3 2 1	We share common values.
5 4 3 2 1	I'm able to explain the purpose or mission of my group.
5 4 3 2 1	I recognize how my own day-to-day activities contribute to the group's purpose or mission.
5 4 3 2 1	My group's conduct is consistent with its stated purpose and values.
5 4 3 2 1	My group has a clear and consistent direction.
5 4 3 2 1	Overall, I find my efforts with the group inspiring.
	Positive Outlook
5 4 3 2 1	I am proud of the contribution my group is making.
5 4 3 2 1	My contribution to the group is recognized.
5 4 3 2 1	We celebrate achievements.
5 4 3 2 1	We have a sense of humor about challenges we face.
5 4 3 2 1	We have a "can do" attitude.
5 4 3 2 1	We resolve conflicts in positive ways.
5 4 3 2 1	We approach challenges as special opportunities, rather than problems.
5 4 3 2 1	I feel optimistic about the future of my group.
5 4 3 2 1	We have fun together.

Scoring the Cultural Climate Test

Add up the individual scores. The maximum score on the test is 100. Few groups achieve this ideal, but you and your peer can use the answers to identify ways to improve the climate. If most individual item scores are 3 or lower, your peer should consider limiting exposure to this group.

With the help of the Cultural Climate Test, your peer can quickly understand the climate concept and how to assess the various social environments in their life. Then the two of you can use these questions to develop a strategy:

- **Do some of your peer's social environments lack a supportive cultural climate?** If "yes," decide whether that is likely to change, what can be done to turn it around, and whether it is best to disengage. Focus on ways to minimize contact with hostile or toxic environments that your peer can't change.

- **Do some of your peer's environments provide a supportive cultural climate?** If "yes," how can your peer benefit more fully from them, and how can people in these settings become involved in supporting your peer's proactive mental health goals?

- **How will your peer find settings with good climates?** Search for positive environments and ask an insider questions like whether people get along and if morale is good. Use the Cultural Climate Test questions as a guide in observing whether a sense of community, a shared vision and a positive outlook are evident. Some environments are difficult to read. In my neighborhood, for example, the annual summer picnic, beach cleanup and neighborhood meeting would be the only times to get a full read on the neighborhood's social climate. You would have to take part in one of these events to fully appreciate the positive spirit of the neighborhood.

Working with Cultural Norms

In a supportive culture, the desired behavior is the normal practice. People would be surprised if you behaved any other way. In a fitness-oriented household culture, for example, housemates would talk about their daily exercise plans and share responsibilities so that everyone got time for physical activity. Housemates would share tips about hiking, biking, and other interests. You would celebrate fitness achievements.

Cultural norms are usually so embedded in the social fabric that we don't notice their influence. If a desired practice is against the norm, people are likely to get concerned, and your peer is likely to hear statements like, "Around here, we don't do it that way." If the desired practice is a norm, the behavior will either meet with approval or go unnoticed. After all, norms are "the way we do things around here."

With your peer, assess the norms in their social environments to determine the level of cultural support for their proactive mental health goal. The following questions may help:

- Which social settings have norms that are for, neutral, or against the proactive mental health goal?

- How can you minimize exposure to groups with unsupportive norms?

- Which groups, if any, already have strong norms that support the proactive mental health goal?

- How can you find or create new groups with supportive norms?

- How can you maximize exposure to groups with supportive norms?

Working with Cultural Touch Points

A culture touches its members in subtle and not-so-subtle ways. If norms represent what is expected of people in a culture, touch points are the social mechanisms that establish and reinforce those expectations. Touch points, like reward systems, reinforce the behavior.

Touch points are often embedded in formal and informal policies and procedures. For example, there may be a formal orientation program for a new employee offered by the human resources department, and there is also likely to be an informal orientation by coworkers that occurs on the job or over lunch.

In a family culture, most of the touch points are informal. For example, a family may discuss nutrition while at the grocery store or at the dinner table. This would be the informal communication system that influences goals for healthy eating.

The following questions examine such cultural influences.

Examining Cultural Touch Points

Instructions: These questions examine how a group, family or organization hinders or promotes the desired proactive mental health behavior. Keep your peer's behavior change goal in mind when discussing answers to the following questions.

Touch Points	Positive Influences	Negative Influences
Rewards and Recognition	Is the proactive mental health behavior rewarded and praised?	Is undesired or unhealthy behavior rewarded and praised?
Modeling	Do leaders model the proactive mental health behavior?	Do leaders model unhealthy behavior?
Pushback	Is unhealthy behavior effectively discouraged or confronted?	Is the proactive mental health behavior discouraged or ridiculed?
Relationships	Do people tend to form relationships while practicing the desired proactive mental health behavior?	Do people form relationships around unhealthy practices?

Learning and Training	Are people offered skills and information needed to excel at the proactive mental health behavior?	Are people offered skills and information that encourage unhealthy practices?
First Impressions	Does the orientation (formal and informal) give a first impression that the proactive mental health behavior is the norm?	Are new people given the impression that unhealthy practices are acceptable?
Communication and Information	Are people given feedback about how they are doing with the proactive mental health behavior?	Is proactive mental health behavior likely to go unnoticed? Are such practices unmeasured and unreported?
Traditions and Symbols	Do celebrations, holidays and special events reflect support for the proactive mental health behavior?	Do celebrations tend to feature unhealthy behavior?

Resource Commitment	Does the use of time, space, or money show that the proactive mental health behavior is important?	Are there inadequate resources available for the proactive mental health behavior?
Story and Narrative	Is the proactive mental health behavior featured in the narrative about the history and future of the group or organization?	Is the proactive mental health behavior either missing from or incompatible with the story of the group/ organization?
Laws and Policies	Do laws, formal policies, and informal rules encourage the proactive mental health behavior?	Do laws, formal policies, and informal rules restrict or work against the proactive mental health behavior?
Goal Setting and Planning	Is proactive mental health taken into consideration when collective goals are set and plans are made?	Are unhealthy behaviors featured in the goals and plans of the group or organization?

Many touch points work together to influence behavior. They can also give contradictory messages. For example, a parent may communicate that he values healthy eating, yet be a poor role model when it comes to healthy eating. Some touch points may be sending no signals. For example, a family may have no discussion of healthy eating.

It takes power and influence to change touch points. If your peer does not have such authority, it is at least helpful to be aware of these influences and to advocate for needed change. If your peer has power, as is often the case within a family, a group of friends or immediate coworkers, then help your peer work with others to adjust the touch points so that they better support proactive mental health goals.

The following ideas are often useful in thinking about adjusting cultural touch points:

- Members of a group or organization may not have examined many of these influences. When these influences are revealed, people may be open to making changes.

- Efforts to change the influences frequently require decision-making authority or the support of those who have such authority. Try to get the decision makers engaged in addressing the touch points.

- It is not necessary to create an entirely new system or to address all the negative influences. We are often better off adjusting existing influences. For example, there may already be a system for rewarding positive practices at work. Encourage your peer to see if proactive mental health behaviors can be recognized within this existing program.

- Start with the influences that will have the biggest impact and are easiest to change. For example, it may be easier for your peer to make changes with their work group or family culture.

Put Subcultures to Work for Proactive Mental Health

Each of your peer's cultural settings contributes to determining the overall influence on their proactive mental health goals. Each setting has its own touch points. For example, the workplace culture may offer predominantly positive influences, whereas the household culture may undermine proactive mental health goals. Ideally, the overall impact will be positive. However, it is likely that one or more settings will not fully support the proactive mental health goal. As with negative norms and dysfunctional cultural climates, your peer will find it helpful to reduce contact with environments that have touch points that work against a proactive mental health goal. Another tactic would be to increase contact with settings that are more likely to have a positive influence.

Checklist for Locating Supportive Environments

Before turning to the next chapter on working through relapse, use the following checklist to determine whether you and your peer have addressed important features of the environment:

- We have explored the possibility of developing buddy relationships around proactive mental health.

- We have looked at physical environments and found ways to make them more supportive of proactive mental health goals.

- We have assessed the cultural climate and have found ways to limit contact with hostile or otherwise unsupportive environments. We have discussed increasing contact with settings that have a strong sense of community, shared vision, and positive outlook.

- We have identified cultural norms that support proactive mental health goals. We have developed a strategy to become immersed in environments where our desired behaviors are "the way we do things around here."

- We have looked at cultural touch points embedded in formal and informal policies and procedures. We have found ways to increase desired influences and to lessen undesirable influences.

Worksheet for Locating Supportive Environments

There are many ways to find or build supportive environments. Ask your peer about their physical and social environments. Answers to the following questions will help you tailor your efforts.

Questions	Commentary
1. Locating Supportive Physical Environments	
What is the ideal place and setup for your new behavior?	Think about a place that is safe, convenient, well-maintained, a desirable temperature, appropriately equipped, affordable and comfortable.
What places support your goal and how can you spend more time in those places?	The right place makes proactive mental health behaviors easier.
What places are unsupportive and how can they be modified or avoided?	It is hard to stick with your goal if a setting is not right.
How can you find or create new supportive places?	New surroundings offer an opportunity to pick places that are specifically chosen for their positive attributes.

2. Mobilizing Proactive Mental Health Buddies

Do your proactive mental health goals lend themselves to partnering with another person?	Almost all proactive mental health goals lend themselves to forming a proactive mental health buddy relationship in which both people pursue the same or similar goals together.
Who might be a good proactive mental health buddy?	Start with existing social networks and housemates and, if necessary, look into support groups, proactive mental health seminars and online resources.
What are the barriers to finding a proactive mental health buddy?	Your peer may need to go beyond their comfort zone to find a potential buddy. Role-play the conversation to get more comfortable. Most people are open to being asked.
What is the best schedule for connecting with proactive mental health buddies?	It is important to coordinate schedules so that proactive mental health buddies can do some of their new practices together.

3. Locating Supportive Cultural Environments	
What social settings, if any, have a climate that is hostile to the desired behavior?	It is important to spend less time in settings that lack a sense of community, a shared vision and a positive outlook. Such settings sap energy and are distracting.
What social settings, if any, have cohesive climates?	It is helpful to increase time in these settings, as they enhance personal functioning and are good sources of social support.
What social settings have cultural norms that fail to support the proactive mental health goal?	If a desired behavior is against the norm, it will be difficult to maintain. Contact with such settings should be limited.
What social settings have norms that support the proactive mental health goal?	If the desired behavior is also the norm, it will be easier to maintain that new behavior. Contact with such settings should be maximized.

What cultural touch points support the proactive mental health goal?	It is helpful to take advantage of touch points that may reward or otherwise endorse desired behavior.
What cultural touch points work against the proactive mental health goal?	Develop strategies to reduce or work around these unsupportive influences.

Chapter 7
Working Through Setbacks

I always wanted to be somebody. If I made it, it's half because I was game enough to take a lot of punishment along the way and half because there were a lot of people who cared enough to help me.

—ALTHEA GIBSON

PROACTIVE MENTAL HEALTH goals can be a great challenge. They involve changes in daily practices and sustained effort. They often require that we overcome ingrained habits, distractions, or chemical addictions, and that we continue despite deep and long-standing psychological wounds. And, as we saw in the last chapter, we are likely to encounter many physical and social obstacles.

Given this, it is hardly surprising that most people do not achieve proactive mental health goals on their first try. Some goals take many attempts before they are achieved.

Your peer must learn how to address the possibility of relapse and how he can move forward beyond the shame and doubt that often accompanies a setback. You can offer support at this important time.

Preventing Setbacks

There are many ways to reduce the risk of relapse. We have learned about several of them in previous chapters. We can avoid relapse by setting meaningful and achievable short-term and long-term goals. We can get the facts and base our goals on the best scientific evidence. We can visualize success and learn from the experience of role models. We can lower daily obstacles to change. We can find or create supportive social and physical environments. Together, these peer support strategies create assets that reduce the likelihood of relapse and failure.

Additional relapse-prevention approaches are aimed at avoiding high-risk situations. These questions can help you and your peer identify approaches to staying on track:

- **Are there places that should be avoided?** An alcoholic beginning recovery should stay away from bars. Identify the equivalent high-risk circumstance for your peer's proactive mental health goal.

- **Are there social circumstances that should be avoided?** Maybe tensions at family gatherings make progress with overeating or stress management unlikely. Identify the groups and social activities that place your peer at risk.

- **Are there times of the day or week that are difficult?** For example, being tired often impairs judgment and willpower. Slow risers may find early morning a time of higher risk. Help your peer identify the most vulnerable times or days so that you can develop strategies for working around them.

- **Are there emotional states that are high risk?** Anger, sadness, and fear often throw us off track. Help your peer identify the triggers for such emotions. Develop strategies for staying on track when these emotions arise.

Checking In

Schedule frequent meetings to discuss progress when your peer is in the early phase of adopting the new proactive mental health behavior. Lag time is an important factor in working though relapse; it is best to get back on track as soon as possible. For example, when I set a goal of cutting back on caffeine, I needed some help soon after my first cappuccino. It was not long thereafter that I slipped back into my undesired practice throughout the day. I might have stuck with my goal if I had a supportive peer help me reexamine my commitment and approach right away.

Even though relapse is common, it need not be inevitable. Do not set an expectation for relapse. Instead, begin a discussion of how to address relapse as a "just in case" plan. Your hope is that your peer will avoid relapse and experience steady progress.

Addressing a Setback

Working through the emotional and physiological fallout of swings in proactive mental health behavior requires great kindness, understanding, creativity and resilience. The following topics make it easier to address the "just in case" of relapse.

Restoring Adult-to-Adult Communication

Feelings of failure tend to make us feel small and guilty – more like a misbehaving child than an adult. Thus, for someone who has experienced relapse, there is a tendency to see others as parents – possibly angry or disappointed parents. This does not make for a good peer support relationship. We cannot be helpful or constructive in this parental role with our peer. No adult finds it satisfying to feel like a child who has misbehaved; such feelings make it likely that your peer will avoid people who treat them like a child.

Effective peer support requires getting back to a conversation between two adult equals. You can bring the relationship back to balance using the following strategies:

1. Make clear that you are not a judge or a parent and that you see your peer as an adult.

2. Remind your peer that relapse is common. You can offer an example of how you got off track during your own past attempts at behavior change.

3. State that your respect does not depend on what your peer decides about continuing their efforts to achieve the proactive mental health goal.

4. State that your immediate goal is to find out what happened, including the facts and the circumstances, and to determine – together – how to proceed.

Interpreting Setbacks

Listen for both facts and feelings. Was this a stumble or a true fall? A person thrown from a horse could get right back on the horse, decide to wait for a better horse, or decide that horseback riding is not such a great idea for them. What scenario fits best? Consider these choices:

- **Maybe this was a stumble, and your peer still sees themself as moving forward.** This would be a good interpretation of the experience because it maintains a sense of momentum. Perhaps there are some lessons that the stumble revealed about avoiding future troubles or about managing such incidents.

- **Maybe your peer views all momentum as lost and believes it is necessary to start over.** If this is the case, express your enthusiasm for a new beginning and use the experience to adjust the strategy and your support.

- **Maybe your peer wants to wait before starting over.** If this is the case, you can acknowledge the decision and return to your peer's initial motivations for making the change. What would tip the balance toward making another go? What factors would determine when to try again?

- **Maybe your peer has had enough of this goal.** If this is the case, you can acknowledge the decision and review possible alternative plans. What changes in goals or strategy make sense? Offer your assistance with any new goal.

Getting Out of a Funk

There is little doubt that a setback can be discouraging. Fortunately, Martin Seligman, Ph.D., a founder of the field of positive psychology, has developed several strategies for regaining optimism. When your peer encounters a problem, they can choose to interpret that problem as a pessimist would or as an optimist would:

An Optimist's Interpretation	A Pessimist's Interpretation
My troubles are not *permanent*. They will soon go away.	My troubles are here to stay. I will always need to put up with this problem.
My troubles are not *pervasive*. This issue is limited in scope.	My troubles will ruin my entire life and spread over into other previously satisfactory things I have done.
My troubles are not *personal*. They are mostly caused by factors that are not my doing.	My troubles are my fault. I brought them upon myself and no one and nothing else is to blame.

Helping your peer move toward the optimist's position

is a useful strategy for raising their spirits after a relapse. Examine the situation to look for reasons the relapse is not permanent, not pervasive and not personal. The strategy only works if your peer believes it is the truth. Look for credible reasons for your peer to take the position of the optimist.

Fortunately, as we have seen throughout this book, there are many external factors that influence behavior change outcomes. They are at least partially responsible for any relapse. Unhealthy behaviors don't have to be permanent. A new, positive interpretation of the event can lift the cloud of failure and shed new light on the situation.

Checklist for Working Through Setbacks

Before turning to the next chapter on celebrating success, see if you and your peer have planned for possible relapse:

- We developed ways to avoid situations that may trigger a relapse.

- We set check-in times so that setbacks can be discussed soon after they happen.

- We affirmed our goal of maintaining an adult-to-adult relationship regardless of how or whether proactive mental health goals are achieved.

- We explored the range of possible setbacks and recognized that we can move forward after a relapse.

- We examined whether our helping relationship was still helping.

Worksheet for Working Through Setbacks

Avoiding setbacks and working through those that occur requires creativity and forethought. Answers to the following questions will help you tailor your efforts.

Questions	Commentary
1. Preventing Setbacks	
What social situations should be avoided?	Some people and social events are triggers for the old behavior. They raise the risk of relapse and should be avoided.
What places should be avoided?	Some places trigger old and unwanted behavior. They raise the risk of relapse and should be avoided.
What times of the day or week are particularly difficult and what can your peer do to pay special attention during these times?	Coping methods can be used to make it easier to get through those times when your peer finds the old behavior most tempting.
What emotional states are high risk and how can they be avoided?	Sadness, anger, frustration, fatigue, and other feelings can throw us off. Plan to limit such mental states and to develop coping strategies.

2. Checking In	
How often will we check in, so that any relapse can be discussed early on?	It is important to stay in touch with your peer to offer encouragement and to address setback issues.
3. Addressing a Setback	
How will we make sure that we maintain adult-to-adult communication?	When a setback occurs, it is common to feel like a misbehaving child. It is important for your peer to quickly return to feeling like an adult.
What is the result of a setback in terms of next steps?	Determine if: (1) the goal has been abandoned, (2) a decision has been made to start over, or (3) a temporary stumble has occurred.
How will we regain optimism and get out of a funk?	A setback can be less draining if it is interpreted as temporary, narrow in its impact, and not entirely your peer's fault.

Chapter 8
Celebrating Success

Celebrate what you want to see more of.

—Tom Peters

Too often, we miss out on acknowledging successes. Unheralded success does more than undercut our good cheer. It is a missed opportunity to reinforce desired practices. This is particularly true with proactive mental health goals in American culture; daily practices are sometimes considered private endeavors and sharing progress might be labeled as bragging.

An unintended side effect of the "go it alone" approach is that no one even knows when benchmarks are set, let alone achieved. In the health-care setting, for example, privacy agreements forbid sharing, even when it's good news.

Advocates of the quiet approach go on to praise the value of self-achievement and self-responsibility, as if help from others somehow taints successful behavior change and downgrades the achievement. "She did it entirely on her own" becomes a special bragging right. I have come to understand, however, that often, when someone "does it on her own," it is a sad sign of a disconnected society and a strong indication that the changes will be short-lived. We want and need to celebrate together.

Celebrating All Along the Way

One of the best things about peer support is that peers can actively seek opportunities to celebrate, and there are many such opportunities. This goes well beyond the typical approach of celebrating only when the ultimate goal is achieved. Consider the possibilities for celebrating success. You can celebrate when:

- Your peer completes the Proactive Mental Health Self-Assessment and determines that they already have many strengths.
- Your peer sets a proactive mental health goal.
- Your peer finds a role model.
- Your peer gets input from the role model. This is also an opportunity to appreciate the role model's input.
- Your peer eliminates one or more barriers to change.
- Your peer finds people and places that will support their proactive mental health goal.

- Your peer develops strategies for limiting contact with unsupportive environments.
- Your peer develops and implements strategies for avoiding setback.
- Your peer gets back on track after a setback.
- It is the anniversary of a significant achievement.

In addition to this list, there are times to celebrate that correspond to the stages of behavior change discussed in Chapter 3, Setting Proactive Mental Health Goals. Each stage has its own transition and marker that can be celebrated. The following table describes these changes in broad terms.

Transitions Included in Prochaska's Stages of Behavior Change

Transition	Marker
From Developing Commitment to Preparation	Date is set for making the change.
From Preparation to Action	Personal changes begin.
From Action to Maintenance	Early adjustment shifts to long-term sustainability.
From Maintenance to Moving On	New lifestyle practice is firmly established and peer is ready to move on to other goals.

Chapter 8

Dividing up behavior change by stages offers several opportunities to celebrate. When your peer moves from thinking about change to setting a time to make that change, it is time to celebrate. When they have finished preparing and begin to make the behavior change, celebrate again. Celebrations are also in order when behavior changes have been successful for a short period. When your peer's changes have taken hold several months or a year into the effort, it is once more time to celebrate.

Tuning in with Intrinsic Rewards

Good celebrations often include rewards. Such rewards come in two forms: intrinsic and extrinsic. An intrinsic reward is a benefit that directly results from behavior change, such as feeling more energetic after becoming fit. An extrinsic reward is a benefit from another source. The 30-day sobriety chip of Alcoholics Anonymous is an example of an extrinsic reward.

Most proactive mental health goals result in multiple intrinsic rewards. Someone with a goal of proactively addressing a breast cancer diagnosis might gain an intrinsic reward of being free from cancer signs and symptoms. They might also learn how to manage great personal threats and challenges. The process and achievements may become a great source of self-discovery and an opportunity to establish new personal priorities. These are all intrinsic rewards.

Explore the intrinsic rewards likely to result from your peer's efforts and ultimate goal achievement. What are all the intrinsic benefits? Achieving proactive mental health goals lowers the probability of getting sick and reduces recovery time. In addition, many behavior changes improve job performance and mood. Your peer's proactive mental health achievements may directly benefit their loved ones. For example, a less agitated parent is likely to benefit a child seeking to get adequate sleep.

Some benefits are surprising. Did you know that stopping smoking improves sexual performance? There is a lot of scientific information about the various health consequences associated with unhealthy and healthy behaviors. You and your peer can review this information to uncover some wonderful rewards.

Getting Rewarded by Others

Extrinsic rewards are the way peers, groups and society reinforce proactive mental health. For example, your peer could reward you for your support with praise, a card or some other form of acknowledgment. Similar informal rewards are available from family, friends and housemates. For example, a man who has lowered his cholesterol might comment that one great reward was the look on his wife's face when he shared the good news with her.

Organizations and society also have rewards for proactive mental health activities, such as incentives for completing company health risk appraisals. Good health could lead to job promotions, since advancement is often linked to personal productivity and people tend to be absent from work or a lot less productive when they are sick. There are also rewards associated with competitions. I appreciate the t-shirts and medals I get for competing in fitness events.

Sometimes extrinsic rewards are criticized because they can distract from intrinsic rewards. Other criticisms concern how external rewards are often temporary and not controlled by the person making the change. It can seem odd or unnecessary to offer external rewards to someone for doing something that offers great intrinsic health benefits.

However, in most cases, it is best to have a powerful mix of intrinsic and extrinsic rewards. For example, stopping smoking is a great accomplishment with direct intrinsic health benefits for those who quit. However, extrinsic rewards, such as lowered health insurance deductibles for nonsmokers, do not undermine the intrinsic rewards. Extrinsic rewards just make the behavior change even more rewarding and can get the attention of people who have yet to pay attention to the intrinsic rewards.

You can help your peer tune in to the intrinsic rewards and make sure that they get all the external perks, pay and praise available for their achievements.

Refining the Reward Systems

As we can see with the list of reasons to celebrate and with the variety of intrinsic and extrinsic rewards available, there are many ways to make celebrations meaningful and appropriate. The following questions to talk with your peer about some of the rewards that would be meaningful to them.

When you celebrate:

- **What level of privacy do you want?** Public disclosure and commitment can work in favor of successful behavior change. It is a lot harder to give up or go back to old habits once your peer has declared their intentions and progress. However, they may not want particular people to know about any changes under way. Who should and should not know? How can you celebrate and yet maintain desired confidentiality?

- **How can you make rewards compatible with proactive mental health?** In American culture, many common rewards are inconsistent with a proactive mental health message. For example, celebrating with alcohol is not consistent with goals for sleeping more soundly. Alcohol interferes with restorative sleep. A massage might be a better choice. We may need to be creative and willing to break with tradition to create a positive reward system for proactive mental health.

- **Are there savings that can finance a grand prize?** When I stopped drinking diet soda and fancy coffees, I put the money into a travel fund. Over a couple of years, these savings made it possible for me to take my grandmother on a cruise to Alaska. See if your peer's achievements offer some cost savings or another financial benefit. Avoiding illness adds to productivity and reduces costs. Can some or all of this money be redirected toward a fitting reward?

- **What are your peer's favorite ways to celebrate?**
We all have our preferences – our favorite way to relax, our favorite healthy foods, our favorite way to exercise, our favorite places. Rewards should be tailored to personal taste. What is the nicest thing anyone ever said to your peer? Maybe the tone and spirit of that comment can be mirrored in how proactive mental health achievements are celebrated. For example, I found it particularly satisfying when my father talked to me in private about how proud he was of my professional achievements. I favor such private acknowledgment of current proactive mental health achievements. Some people find monetary rewards most meaningful. If this is the case, see if a family member would be willing to reward change with cash or a check, or if there are financial incentives available from their employer.

- **Are there special people to celebrate with?** Perhaps certain esteemed friends, family members or coworkers would offer particularly meaningful rewards to your peer – intrinsic or otherwise. Expressions of delight from a spouse, a "way to go" from the boss, or praise from parents may carry special weight.

Finishing Strong

If you and your peer have organized your efforts in the same sequence as in this book, then you may be reaching a good check-in point for your proactive mental health efforts. Presumably you have discussed and worked with the six primary peer support strategies of goal setting, identifying role models, eliminating barriers to change, locating supportive environments, working through relapse and, with this chapter, celebrating success.

Now it is time to take stock of your relationship:

- Spend a few moments in appreciation of your time together, the trust you have maintained, your commitment to success and your ability to adapt.

- Discuss what each of you has learned in terms of peer support and how best to approach behavior change in the future.

- Decide how you will work together in the future. Include in this conversation any new goals to consider, time commitments, and any other adjustments. For example, you may decide that by a certain date it would be a good time to meet less frequently, or to change your check-in format to phone calls and e-mails.

- Find a way to celebrate your relationship. This celebration could take the form of a symbol of your appreciation or a special meal or a shared fun event.

Checklist for Celebrating Success

The following checklist helps determine if you have a good plan for celebrating success:

- We have identified several times to celebrate milestones and achievements.

- We have compiled a comprehensive list of intrinsic rewards (such as health and well-being benefits) that are likely to occur if the efforts are successful.

- We have identified extrinsic rewards (such as pay, bonuses and gifts) that will be available because of the proactive mental health effort.

- We have discussed strategies for tailoring celebrations and rewards so they are appropriate and meaningful.

- We have celebrated our relationship by checking in and by honoring our time together.

Worksheet for Celebrating Success

How can you help your peer avoid the all-too-common mistake of missing opportunities to celebrate. Answers to the following questions will help you tailor your efforts.

Questions	Commentary
1. Celebrating All Along the Way	
Have we identified several reasons to celebrate?	Overlooking successes can undermine positive energy. It is important to look for the many opportunities to acknowledge your peer's proactive mental health efforts.
What are the markers for the transitions in the stages of behavior change, and how will we recognize and acknowledge these transitions?	The six stages of behavior change offer a roadmap for focusing your peer's efforts; moving one stage forward deserves a celebration.
2. Identifying Intrinsic Rewards	
What are the health and quality-of-life rewards for your peer when they achieve their proactive mental health goal?	Such benefits include feeling more energetic, increasing personal performance, reducing a health risk, healing, and living longer. Some benefits will be obvious, and others may require a review of the scientific literature.

How might your peer's success benefit others?	Many proactive mental health goals benefit others. This benefit may be important to your peer.
3. Identifying Extrinsic Rewards	
How will your peer's successful behavior change be acknowledged by others?	Lowered health risk and positive practices sometimes trigger extrinsic rewards such as career advancement, financial savings, and praise. Your peer may need to apply for such payoffs.
4. Refining the Reward System	
What degree of privacy is desired with rewards?	Some people are less comfortable with public acknowledgment, so their rewards need to be low-key. Others thrive on external acknowledgement.
How will we make rewards compatible with proactive mental health?	Standard rewards may be inconsistent with a proactive mental health message, so you may need to create more healthful strategies.

Will your peer experience financial savings from the behavior change, and can this money be incorporated into a reward?	Savings are easy to see if the old practice cost money. Also factor in less obvious savings such as time, fewer absences, and reduced health care.
Are there special people who should be involved with the rewards for achieving proactive mental health goals?	Family members, friends and mentors could add meaning to rewards by being involved with acknowledgment of your peer's change.

5. Finishing Strong

What has been useful and enjoyable about the peer support relationship?	Reflect on the positive qualities of the relationship, how it evolved, how you overcame challenges, and what you accomplished.
How will you celebrate your relationship?	Take time to recognize your relationship and how it has enriched both of your lives.

Chapter 9
A Call to Kindness

What wisdom can you find that is greater than kindness?

—Jean-Jacques Rousseau

At this point in *Better Together*, you have read about and hopefully experienced the power of effective peer support in bringing about lasting and positive behavior change. Peer support weaves together the mental health domains of personal behavior and social connection. By enhancing the quality and quantity of social support, we increase the likelihood of success. Furthermore, efforts to offer effective support enhance human connections. Traditionally, helping people with behavior change has been primarily the domain of the therapist and wellness professional. I believe that extending this helping role to our peers can be a catalyst for a proactive mental health revolution.

Cleaning the Poisoned Cultural Well

Most epidemics can be traced to a source. The classic public health example is a poisoned well in London. The people in the vicinity of the Broad Street pump were getting sick. John Snow, a London physician, figured this out and removed the pump's handle; the illness vanished.

When it comes to unhealthy behavior, cultural environments are the most likely source. The culture is the poisoned well. Social media platforms and video games too often spread hate and teach violence. Bars, parties and alcohol ads have their role in making people susceptible to substance abuse.

Is proactive mental health a pipedream? Is it possible to be sane in a world gone mad? Given the rapid rise in mental illness, it is clear that we are heading in the wrong direction. The many negative influences in North American culture make it tempting to tell people to go it alone – it's just too hard to get support to do what you want to do. But, just as the residents of London could not do without another source of water, humans require social contact to survive and thrive. Proactive mental health attitudes and practices can have social roots. Those who exercise regularly, for example, probably learned and were encouraged in developing their fitness skills through a coach, family member or friend. The question is not really whether we will have social contact, but rather whether this contact supports our mental well-being.

The vision of creating a proactive mental health culture was born out of necessity. Our mental health problems are exploding. Our treatment options are limited. We can't afford a larger bill. In a tight labor market, we can't just push mental illness under the rug. We need to strengthen our defenses and lower our risk of debilitating mental conditions.

Peer Support Could Bring a Better Future

Where and when do we address mental health needs? At first glance, peer support seems like an unlikely place to begin. Many people are reluctant to discuss their personal problems. Most peers are uncomfortable assisting with their mental illness challenges. Helping people address personal problems has its limitations.

But we can build islands of sanity in an otherwise complicated world. We can co-create social environments that reduce the stressors likely to make people sick. In addition, a proactive mental health culture will enhance resilience and grit. And we can build our peer support capacity. We can develop the skills and tools needed to handle future proactive mental challenges.

Can we create a safe harbor among our peers? We can do this together. *Better Together* provides a roadmap and strategies for supporting a friend, family member or coworker to improve their proactive mental health. By adopting proactive mental health behaviors and attitudes, we can reduce the burden of anxiety, depression and other illnesses while enjoying the well-being benefits of living to our full potential.

Connecting

Throughout this book, I have explained how people can help each other achieve proactive mental health goals. Using peer support techniques, you and your peer can make dramatic and lasting behavior changes. Together, you can achieve success rates that would not be possible without support.

If this book has any role in your success, then it was well worth writing. But the very act of people coming together has a benefit that may far exceed the health benefits and personal satisfaction described here. There is strong evidence that human connection is, in and of itself, as powerful a positive life force as any health behavior. The very act of reaching out to help someone in constructive ways enhances your own health and the health of your peer. And the connections you are making enhance the well-being of your workplace, family, and community.

Kindness Makes Us Great

Better Together is a call to kindness. Hopefully this book will make peer support more comfortable, more effective, and more available. The idea of learning to give and receive effective peer support is a new idea that goes beyond the typical self-help approach. The peer support discussed in *Better Together* is many notches up from the informal peer support that most of us have experienced. As with any new idea, you will need to reach out and explain to others how this form of peer support works. You should soon have some successful experiences to share. Real-life stories tend to be persuasive.

Please reach out to your peers when you see them struggling with personal change. Lend them your copy of this book and encourage them to get support. Show a peer how to support you when you need it. In my experience, mutual support and kindness are among the most powerful and important ways to achieve proactive mental health. We are not alone. Our need for one another is not a burden, but rather one of the most enjoyable human experiences. We can achieve great things together.

End Notes

Chapter 1

Merriam-Webster, "Flourish." *Merriam-Webster.com Dictionary.*
https://www.merriam-webster.com/dictionary/flourish. Accessed 24 May, 2022.

American Psychological Association, "Stress in America™ 2020," APA.org. *https://www.apa.org/news/press/ releases/stress/2020/report-october.*

National Institute of Mental Health Statistics. https:// *www.nimh.nih.gov/health/statistics/mental-illness.*

Mental Health First Aid from National Council for Mental Wellbeing. *https://www.mentalhealthfirstaid. org/2019/02/5-surprising-mental-health-sta- tistics/#:~:-text=In%20the%20United%20 States%2C%20*
almost,equivalent%20to%2043.8%20million%20people.

The Lancet Commissions, Vol. 392, Issue 10157, 1553- 1598, October 27, 2018.

"Mental Health for global prosperity: We cannot afford to ignore the impact of mental health on the global economy." *Policy Brief.* Mental Health Innovation Network, Centre for Global Mental Health, London, UK: London School of Hygiene & Tropical Medicine, 2019.

Maddy Reinert, Theresa Nguyen and Danielle Fritze. 2021. *The State of Mental Health in America.* Mental Health American, Inc. 2020. National Institute for Mental Health on Caring for Your Mental Health (2022). *https://www.nimh.nih.gov/ health/topics/ caring-for-your-mental-health.*

World Health Organization's Definition of Health. (2022). https://www.who.int/news-room/fact-sheets/detail/ mental-health-strengthening-our-response#:~:text= The%20WHO%20constitution%20states%3A%20 %22Health,of%20mental%20disorders%20or%20 disabilities.

"Mental Health: Culture, Race, and Ethnicity: A Supplement to Mental Health." *A Report of the Surgeon General.* Office of the Surgeon General (US); Center for Mental Health Services (US); National Institute of Mental Health (US). Rockville (MD): Substance Abuse and Mental

Health Services Administration (US); 2001 Aug.

Fabius R, Frazee S, Thayer D, Kirshenbaum D, Reynolds J. "The Correlation of a corporate culture of health assessment score and health care cost trends." *J Occupational Health Environ Med.* 2018; 60:507–514.

Flynn J, Gascon G, Doyle S, et al. "Supporting a culture of health in the workplace: a review of evidence-based elements." *Am J Health Promotion.* 2018;32:1755–1788.

Terry, PE, Seaverson, EL, Gossmeier J, Anderson Dr. "Association between nine quality components and Make Proactive Mental Health Transformational superior worksite health management results." *J Occupational Health Environ Med.* 2008.

Henke R, Head M, Kent K, Goetzel R, Roemer E, McCleary K. "Improvements in an organization's culture of health reduces workers' health risk profile and health care utilization." *J Occupational Health Environ Med.* 2019; 61:96–101.

Kent K, Goetzel R, Roemer E, et al. "Developing two cultures of health measurement tools. Examining employers' efforts to influence population health inside and outside company walls." *J Occupational Health Environ Med.* 2018; 60:1087–1097.

Pellmar TC, Brandt EN, Baird MA. "Health and behavior: The interplay of biological, behavioral, and social influences: Summary of the Institute of Medicine report." *Am J Health Promotion.* 2002; 16:206-219.

Dean Ornish (1998). *Love & Survival: The Scientific Basis for the Healing Power of Intimacy.* New York: Harper Collins.

Robert F. Allen, Harry N. Dubin, Saul Pilnick, and Adella C. Youtz (1970). *Collegefields: From Delinquency to Freedom.* Special Child Publications, Inc., Seattle Washington.

Sara Harris & Robert F. Allen (1978). *The Quiet Revolution: The Story of a Small Miracle in American Life.* Rawson Associates Publishers, Inc., New York.

Robert F. Allen with Charlotte Kraft (1980). Beat the System! A Way to Create More Human Environments. New York, McGraw-Hill Book Company.

Robert F. Allen with Shirley Linde (1981). *Lifegain: The Exciting New Program that Will Change Your Health and Your Life.* New York: Appleton-Century-Crofts.

Robert F. Allen, Charlotte Kraft, Judd Allen, and Barry Certner (1987). *The Organizational Unconscious: How to Create the Corporate Culture You Want and Need.* Burlington, Vermont, Human Resources Institute Press.

Judd Allen, *(2022). We Flourish: A Guide to Supporting Proactive Mental Health at Work.* Burlington, Vermont, Human Resources Institute Press.

Judd Allen, *(2008). Healthy Habits, Helpful Friends: How to Effectively Support Wellness Lifestyle Goals.* Burlington, Vermont, Human Resources Institute Press.

Judd Allen, *(2008). Wellness Leadership: Creating Supportive Environments for Healthier and More Productive Employees.* Burlington, Vermont, Human Resources Institute Press.

Judd Allen, *(2010). Bringing Wellness Home: Embracing the Power of Supportive Cultural Environments in Your Household.* Burlington, Vermont, Human Resources Institute Press.

Judd Allen & Donald B. Ardell, *(2017). Leading for Purpose: How to Help Your People and Your Organization Benefit from the Pursuit of Purpose.* Burlington, Vermont, Human Resources Institute Press.

Chapter 2

Judd Allen, *(2008). Wellness Leadership: Creating Supportive Environments for Healthier and More Productive Employees.* Burlington, Vermont, Human Resources Institute Press.

Homer. *The Odyssey.* London and New York: W. Heinemann; G.P. Putnam's Sons, 1919.

Chapter 3

James O. Prochaska, John C. Norcross, & Carlo C. DiClemente, PhD (1997). *Changing for Good: A Revolutionary Six-Stage Program for Overcoming Bad Habits and Moving Your Life Positively Forward.* New York, Harper Collins.

Chapter 5

Nelson Mandela (1995). *Long Walk to Freedom.* New York, Abacus/Little Brown Publishers.

Allen R.F. and Allen J (1987). "A sense of community, a shared vision and a positive culture: Core enabling factors in successful culture-based health promotion." *Am J Health Promotion.* Vol. 1, No. 3, pp. 40-47.

Chapter 7

Thomas A Harris, (1969). *I'm ok you're ok: A practical guide to transactional analysis.* New York, Harper & Row.

Martin E.P. Seligman (2006). Learned Optimism: How to change your mind and your life. New York: Vintage Books.

Chapter 8

James O. Prochaska, John C. Norcross, & Carlo C. DiClemente, PhD (1997). *Changing for Good: A Revolutionary Six-Stage Program for Overcoming Bad Habits and Moving Your Life Positively Forward.* New York, Harper Collins.

Chapter 9

Dean Ornish (1998). *Love & Survival: The Scientific Basis for the Healing Power of Intimacy.* New York: Harper Collins.

Sandra Hempel (2007). *The Strange Case of the Broad Street Pump: John Snow and the Mystery of Cholera.* Oakland, California, University of California Press.

About the Author

Judd Allen earned his Ph.D. in community psychology from New York University. He is president of the Human Resources Institute, HealthyCultureNow, LLC and an editor of *the American Journal of Health Promotion*. His previous books include *We Flourish, Wellness Leadership, Culture Change Planner, Bringing Wellness Home, Kitchen Table Talks for Wellness, 103 Challenges for Manager-Led Wellness*, and *Healthy Habits Helpful Friends*. He lives in Burlington, Vermont and Montreal, Canada.

www.ingramcontent.com/pod-product-compliance
Lightning Source LLC
Chambersburg PA
CBHW041711260326
41914CB00038B/1989/J